More Landscape Projects

SIMPLE STEPS TO BEAUTIFY YOUR YARD AND GARDEN

TIME-LIFE BOOKS, ALEXANDRIA, VIRGINIA

More Landscape Projects

Introduction

The next time you see a beautiful landscape, take a close look and you'll see that it is made up of components—such as plantings, paths, and structures—that fit together into a harmonious whole. The projects in this book will help you enhance the different parts of your own landscape and make your entire yard and garden more beautiful.

Every part of your yard holds possibilities for improvement. You may decide to create outdoor floors by installing new walkways or a patio, define your boundaries more agreeably with a fence and plantings, establish shade with an arbor or a pergola, or make more effective spaces for recreation and entertainment by building an outdoor grill or creating a secret garden room. Detailed step-by-step photos and instructions, as well as useful tips, guide you through each project, so you don't need to be an expert, nor do you need fancy equipment or a green thumb to create the many inspiring projects you'll see here.

Because there are often several ways to fulfill the same need, the projects often include two alternatives that illustrate different possibilities or variations on the theme. In addition, complete plant and materials lists help you organize your project and obtain all the supplies and equipment you need to be successful.

Transforming outdoor spaces is not an overnight process. But by carefully studying and following the projects in this book, you'll be on your way toward creating a home landscape that will long be a source of pride and pleasure. ❧

Getting Started

IN THIS SECTION:

Starting a landscape project begins with a plan that takes into account the unique natural features of your site, such as its slope and drainage, as well as its exposure to sunlight and wind. The plan should also consider existing or planned buildings, fences, and other structures. This section will help you analyze these features and decide whether to work with them as they are or modify them.

As you plan your project, you will choose the materials to use—shrubs, trees, and flowers as well as "hardscape" materials such as brick and wood. This section describes a range of materials and their uses, so you can select the one that best suits your project. It also covers techniques for working with them correctly, to ensure both your safety and the longevity of the finished project.

As you accomplish the projects in this book, you will learn new skills—or enhance existing ones—including carpentry, masonry, and garden design. Using the right tools saves time and effort and helps you get the results you expect. This section describes tools used throughout the book. Some you will want to invest in because you will use them many times, and others you will want to rent rather than buy. ❦

Planning Your Project

Landscape projects solve problems so your landscape works better for you. Thorough planning before you launch the project helps ensure that you achieve the outcomes you want.

A detailed map of the area where you plan to build the project is a helpful tool. Map out the surrounding areas also, so you can see how the project might affect them. For example, a new planting or a renovated patio might change the flow of foot traffic or alter drainage patterns. You can use the site map you received when you bought the house, or draw your own after measuring the property. On the map, mark the dimensions of the area, note structures, include plantings, and indicate unique features such as slopes and low spots. You may want to photograph the area as well as drawing a map.

Map which areas are sunny and shaded and include the direction of prevailing winds. Once you have the map, you can draw out different plans on tissue paper, trying out several until you find which one works best.

Do some research before you get started. There are plenty of places to find inspiration and guidance, including home improvement centers, professional consultants, books, magazines, and people who have done similar projects. ❧

YOUR YARD'S CONDITIONS

When planning your project, it is vital that you evaluate the conditions of your landscape and get to know the unique sites within your yard in terms of light and water.

Be sure to assess drainage in your yard at several times of the year. While some places are constantly moist, others vary from season to season. Good drainage is essential for most plants and all structures.

Also, track sun and shade at different times of the day and throughout the year, since the amount of sunlight an area receives varies not only with the time of day but also with the season. The angle of the sun changes throughout the year. A spot that is shady in the low-angled sunlight of winter may be brightly lit in summer.

Match your plant choices to the conditions in your yard. When planting, check the tags or consult a reference book for light requirements. A plant labeled full sun needs at least six hours of direct sun per day to thrive. Partial sun means four to six hours of direct sun (preferably in the morning, as afternoon sun is hotter), and shade means fewer than four hours of sun per day. ❧

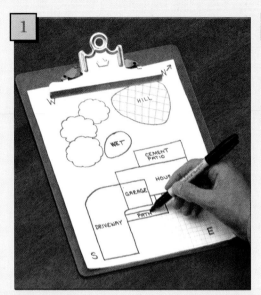

Make a map of the area as it appears before beginning the project. Include natural and artificial features, such as plants and buildings.

Label and list in order of importance areas that need improvement in your landscape. These may include wet spots and worn pathways.

Explore potential solutions, searching for the one with the most benefits. For example, a fence creates privacy, blocks wind, and serves as a trellis.

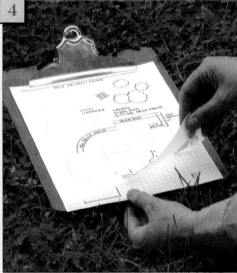

To see how the completed project will work in the yard, make a scale plan of it on tissue paper and overlay it on the landscape map.

Choosing Materials

The choice of materials you use in your landscape involves balancing design considerations with practical goals. You want the materials to coordinate with the style of your house, harmonize well with the neighborhood, and also be within your budget. And you'll find both the work and the result more enjoyable if you use materials that suit your skills and physical ability.

The setting will influence your choice of materials, too. For example, a rustic wood gate that opens to a curving mulched pathway is a natural choice for a shady woodland yard. The more formal look of a brick walkway laid in a highly organized pattern makes more sense in a sunny front yard with a strongly symmetrical design.

As you study the projects in this book, think about how different landscape features may help you to achieve a more unified look. One strategy that works well is to choose a single dominant building material, for example, flagstone or a certain wood, and use it repeatedly in your landscape plan.

When planning ahead, remember to consider what you already have to work with in your landscape. Trees can be sculpted into more pleasing forms with careful pruning, and stark fences can be softened with evergreen shrubs or flowering vines. You may not like the concrete walkway that leads to your front door, but it can be enhanced with tile or replaced by brick pavers or mortared stone for beautiful and lasting results.

The following pages present an overview of the various materials you might choose for new landscape features, starting with brick, stone, and concrete, and then wood. You will also find tips and techniques for working with these materials and the tools that make it easier to achieve success.

Remember, some landscape features are planted rather than built. Trees, shrubs, vines, and colorful flowers can become features in themselves, or you can use them to enhance the appearance of other landscape elements. You will find suggestions for dependable plants for various uses, but you should also solicit advice from a local nursery professional before investing in long-lived plants for your yard. 🌾

METAL ACCENTS. *Introduce drama, strength, and durability by using classic wrought iron, copper, or plastic-coated steel.*

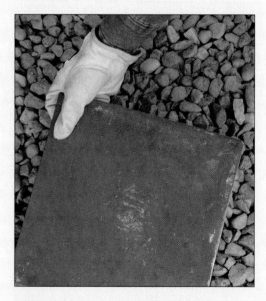

TILE. *Whether used as steppingstones or a patio floor, tile adds color, beauty, and flair to your home landscape.*

PLASTIC LUMBER. *Unlike wood, this new material never rots or splinters, and it requires very little, if any, maintenance.*

VINYL. *Fences, railings, and even garden furniture of vinyl don't rust, rot, or splinter, are easy to clean, and never need painting.*

PLANTING TREES AND SHRUBS. *Loosen and remove burlap wrapping from rootball of balled-and-burlapped plants.*

SHOPPING FOR PERENNIALS. *Choose plants with well-grown healthy-looking tops and strong root systems.*

HERE'S HOW

DESIGN IDEAS

Look into your neighbors' yards to see how they have used various building materials. By sticking with materials that already exist in nearby properties, you can create a landscape that is in harmony with the neighborhood. This is especially important if you anticipate selling your house in the future. What kind of fences do you see in adjoining backyards? Do front yards have something in common, such as brick walkways, lampposts, or a certain type of tree? Getting advice from the neighbors has its practical side as well. People who have already solved challenging landscape problems are usually happy to share what they learned in the process.

Understanding Drainage

GRADING NEAR HOUSE. *Spread topsoil around foundations to replace eroded soil. The soil should slope slightly away from the house.*

It's a natural law that water runs downhill. And in places where water cannot readily be absorbed by the ground, it tends to run in great volume. Houses, driveways, walkways, and other hard surfaces increase runoff, which, in turn, can create problems with drainage. Not all properties have drainage problems, but it's still something to look into early in your efforts to develop the landscape. Water that collects around foundations can cause flooding or long-term damage, such as rotting or insect infestation. And it's not just buildings that may suffer. Many plants will not tolerate constantly soggy soil.

To assess drainage problems, study your yard during a heavy rain and again an hour after the rain has stopped. Large puddles, mud collecting in walkways, and places where grass and soil are clearly washing away are clues to trouble. You have a serious problem if your whole yard turns into a pond, but poor drainage is more likely to appear in small areas where water from gutters and paved areas naturally tends to flow.

In addition to grading problems, soil type affects drainage, too. Water flows through sandy soil much faster than through clay. If your soil is high in clay, the cycle of wet and dry causes the ground to expand and contract, which can harm structures and plants. You can minimize the problem by applying mulch to help hold in moisture. It also may help to working some compost into the soil. Underground, hard layers of rock or compacted subsoil can also contribute to drainage problems.

If you identify a poorly drained area, the first solution is to try to make the wet area attractive by turning it into a boggy garden. If living with a wet area isn't an option, you can regrade the spot or install special pipes to help channel unwanted water away.

HAVE ON HAND:

- Topsoil
- Garden rake
- Shovel
- Pebbles for mulch
- Downspout extensions
- Compost
- Grass seed
- Straw for mulch

A BERM. *Created by making a raised area of soil, a berm can slow the movement of water while redirecting its flow.*

EROSION PROTECTION. *To reduce erosion where you expect a heavy flow of drainage water, add a 3- or 4-inch layer of small stones.*

DOWNSPOUTS. *If you have gutters, prevent problems by adding downspout extensions that steer runoff away from the house.*

A SWALE. *Lined with water-tolerant plants or stone, these depressions, like dry streambeds, control erosion while accenting the landscape.*

REPAIRING LOW SPOTS. *Fill the depression with compost, and reseed with lawn grass. Gently tamp soil, water it, and cover with mulch.*

HERE'S HOW

TEST FOR DRAINAGE

Perform a simple test to check your soil drainage. Dig a hole 18 to 24 inches deep and 18 to 24 inches across. Fill it with water. If the water disappears from the hole in 10 minutes or less, you have decent drainage and soil that probably contains a fair amount of sand. If the water takes an hour or more to drain, you may have drainage problems and soil that contains a large amount of clay. Follow the suggestions outlined on these pages to improve the drainage in such a situation.

A Guide to Stone, Brick, and Concrete

Walkways, landings, and patios paved with a smooth, hard surface are attractive, permanent, and easy to maintain. The more foot traffic an area gets, the stronger the case becomes for a walking surface made of stone, brick, or concrete. And when brick or stone is used for walking surfaces, additional features such as low walls or raised beds constructed of the same material always look like perfectly matched pieces of a cohesive whole.

The primary access route from your car to your door should be constructed with safety in mind, which almost always means using one of these materials underfoot. Some sites, however, are not suitable for paving of any kind. Where drainage is already poor, increasing the amount of area with a hard surface may make it worse. You may want to consider using loose stone in such a site. Also, avoid paving near trees with shallow roots, such as sugar maple or beech, which is as detrimental to the trees as it is to the walkway or patio.

Though stone, brick, and concrete are used in comparable ways and can even look similar, the materials aren't the same. The concrete of finished paths and patios is as hard as rock, but it didn't begin that way. Concrete is a combination of water and a cementing material, most often Portland cement, and an aggregate such as sand. These materials blend together to form a mixture that can be poured directly on a bed of prepared sand or into preformed plastic molds. Concrete is easy to prepare and can be accented with smooth pebbles to create mosaics or mixed with small stones to form a decorative finish unavailable in brick or stone. Pavers are small blocks made of concrete and used like bricks to surface a walkway, path, or patio.

Bricks are made of clay that has been fire hardened in a kiln. The bricks made for outdoor use have been specially prepared to withstand the rigors of the changing seasons and are resistant to flaking and breakage.

Stone comes in a wide range of colors, shapes, and durability. Fieldstone is irregularly shaped flat rock gathered from many different sources and is excellent for informal walkways. Cut stone is sliced into uniform dimensions, providing a more formal appearance for patios and paths.

As long as you can handle some heavy lifting, working with hard materials is fast and reasonably easy. ❧

PLAIN-FINISH CONCRETE. *Concrete can be poured into preformed molds bought from building suppliers, or you can fabricate your own.*

INTERLOCKING PAVERS. *Made from durable concrete in a range of colors and shapes, these pavers are decorative and easy to install.*

CONCRETE PAVING STONES. *These come in a range of styles and colors, such as the Roman style shown here.*

BRICK PAVERS. *Used on walkways, brick pavers are denser than regular bricks and less prone to breakage and weathering.*

FIELDSTONE AND FLAGSTONE. *For natural beauty that is exceptionally durable, stone is always appropriate.*

PEBBLES AND GRAVEL CHIPS. *These are used to make paths and correct drainage problems. For variety, use colorful ones.*

HERE'S HOW
PROTECT YOUR BACK

Working on an outdoor home improvement project is no fun if you injure yourself. Often it is your back that pays the price for weekend gardening. Here's how to stay ache-free when handling heavy materials:

- Warm up before you get started. Do some gentle twisting from the waist, along with a few easy side bends.
- Do not attempt to lift a heavy object by bending over with your legs straight. Squat down and get as close to the object as possible. Grab hold, and lift by pushing yourself (and the object) up with your legs. By doing this, you'll use your larger, stronger leg muscles, rather than those in your back and arms.
- Invest in a protective belt to support your lower back, if necessary.
- And remember, if it's too heavy or awkward to lift, ask for help!

Working with Stone, Brick, and Concrete

In order for a patio, walkway, or other hard surface to remain smooth and level for years to come, substantial site preparation is usually needed. Concrete will mold itself to the earthen bed where it is poured, but bricks or stones need an excavated bed lined with a 4- to 6-inch layer of crushed rock and a 1- to 2-inch layer of sand. It is important that the ground under the new hard surface be firm, so tamp each layer with a piece of 4 x 4 lumber, a wooden fence post, or a small tamper. In dry climates with soils that have a lot of clay, rock, or sand, a sand base may be all that is necessary, so

TO SET A POST, dig a hole three times the diameter of the post and 1/3 the length plus 6 inches. Tamp bottom of hole until firm.

HAVE ON HAND:

- ▶ Tape measure
- ▶ Post
- ▶ Shovel or post-hole digger
- ▶ Tamper
- ▶ Gravel or crushed stone
- ▶ Fast-setting concrete mix
- ▶ Carpenter's level
- ▶ Wood braces and nails
- ▶ Chalk
- ▶ Chisel
- ▶ Sledgehammer

check with your local building official to see what is required in your area.

If you are installing a walkway or patio with pavers that will not be mortared together, it is a good idea to lay a sheet of landscape fabric between the prepared bed and the pavers, to keep weeds from growing through the crevices. If you desire mortar between bricks or pavers, purchase a mortar mix that requires only the addition of water. Mortar is a mixture of cement, lime, and sand; it differs from concrete in that it retains water and slows down the hardening process.

All hard surfaces should have a very slight slope to aid in the runoff of water. Because the water runs off in sheets, edge the hard surfaces with plants that readily make use of the extra water.

Before you begin, make sure that you have a detailed understanding of how each project will proceed. Do not attempt to handle large expanses of concrete or other hard surfaces by yourself. Get professional help with areas that are more than 12 feet square. You may need to prepare a special area where bricks or stone can be placed during construction, such as a piece of plywood placed over an area of lawn. ❧

TO CUT BRICK, measure the area to be filled, and then transfer the measurement to the brick. Mark the cut line with chalk.

Place 6 inches of gravel in hole and set post in hole. Pour in dry, fast-setting concrete mix to 3 to 4 inches from top.

Check the post for plumb, and brace as needed. Add water to the dry mix per label directions and allow it to soak in. Fill hole with soil.

Use a small chisel and sledgehammer to score the line, making a groove about ⅛ inch deep completely around the brick.

Set the scored brick on a flat surface. Put blade of wide chisel in groove, and tap chisel several times with sledge until brick splits.

HERE'S HOW
CONCRETE COMMON SENSE

Wear heavy rubber gloves, sturdy boots, pants, and a long-sleeved shirt to protect your skin from exposure to wet concrete, which is highly caustic and can burn your skin. It's also a good idea to wear safety glasses when working with concrete to prevent any from splashing into your eyes. In addition, when you are mixing concrete, wear a dust mask to keep from inhaling the dust. If you get any concrete on your skin, whether directly or through soaked clothing, wash promptly with water. If you get any in your eyes, flush them immediately with water and consult a physician.

Remember that concrete hardens through a chemical reaction and becomes harder with age. Have forms in place before you mix it. Keep tools organized and close by so you can work quickly and safely when placing wet concrete.

A Guide to Wood

Useful for building everything from fences to seating, wood is naturally warm and appropriate in most landscapes. If your house has a wood deck, a wood gate, or other wood feature in one part of the yard, using wood in another landscape project helps tie the two features together and make the whole yard more consistent and unified.

Building with wood is fast and economical, but some long-term maintenance is required. Be sure to repair splinters or broken hardware promptly, and repaint every few years to keep wood looking good and protect it from the elements.

Many types of wood can be used for landscape projects. Some woods, such as cypress, cedar, and locust, are naturally resistant to rot. The fine grain and smooth surface of cedar and cypress make them popular for decks, arbors, trellises, and pergolas. Locust is excellent for fencing, especially split rail fences, where the wood's rough grain gives the posts and rails a rugged quality. Rot-resistant woods can be sealed with a nontoxic preservative to maintain the natural color of the wood while increasing its resistance to decay. Or they can be left to weather naturally, gradually turning a soft shade of driftwood gray.

Softwoods such as pine, fir, Douglas fir, and spruce are easy to work with, have attractive natural color and texture, and are often less expensive than cypress and cedar. Because softwoods are not rot resistant, they must be sealed with a nontoxic preservative. For best results, apply sealant after making any cuts so that all surfaces are protected. If you do not want the wood to weather naturally, paint it promptly to preserve it for the longest possible time. Any wood can be stained or painted to the desired tint or color to complement your house and landscape, or a clear sealant can be applied. If you plan to paint your project, paint it with a primer first. Otherwise, the paint will crack and peel as the wood expands and contracts with changes in moisture and temperature. For best results, use high-quality paint, and do the job when the weather is warm and dry.

Because wood deteriorates when exposed to moisture, no wood should be placed in direct contact with the ground. The moisture in the soil causes it to rot and can attract termites. For instance, if you use wood posts to support gates or fences, be sure to set them in concrete. Or, install concrete footers in the ground, and bolt the wood structure in place. 🌼

SPLIT RAIL WOODEN FENCE. *Create this classic with posts and rails that come precut at building supply stores.*

MULCH. *Decorative and practical, mulch such as wood chips or shredded bark is useful for making pathways and setting off trees and flowers.*

LANDSCAPE TIMBERS. *Planed or rough-sawn, sized from 4 x 4 to 12 x 12, timbers can make raised beds, walkways, steps, and terraces.*

PRUNINGS FROM TREES. *Use these to make a rustic trellis, arbor, or fence or to create natural supports for vegetables and flowers.*

LATTICE PANELS. *Sold in 4 x 8-foot pieces, lattice makes easy-to-install screening. Coat panels with a sealant, paint, or stain.*

PRECUT WOOD FENCING PANELS. *Install fences quickly and easily. All you need to do is set posts and then hang the panels.*

HERE'S HOW
TREATED WOOD

Wood that is treated with CCA (chromated copper arsenate) may leach chemicals into soil. This is a particular concern where you are growing vegetables and herbs, because plants can absorb those chemicals. You should not use this wood where skin may come into contact with it, such as for picnic tables or children's play sets. Among many alternatives to treated lumber are naturally rot-resistant cedar, cypress, and locust and manufactured materials such as recycled plastic lumber and vinyl fencing.

If you must use treated wood, look for treatments that do not contain arsenic and chromium or other metals.

Never use railroad ties or old telephone poles that have been treated with toxic creosote.

If you have to handle any treated wood, wear a mask, gloves, and long sleeves to protect your skin from contact with harmful chemicals. Do not burn pressure-treated wood.

Working with Wood

MAKING CLEAN CORNERS. *Use a miter box to hold wood in position and a backsaw with specialized teeth to make a clean cut.*

Top-grade materials and accurate measurements are the keys to successfully working with wood. Carpenters have a famous saying: Measure twice and cut once. If you are new to working with wood, never forget this hard-learned advice.

Buy the highest-quality lumber you can find, and inspect each piece for warping, twisting, splitting, large knotholes, and other flaws. Some imperfections may be only cosmetic, but others will compromise the integrity of your project. Don't be afraid to ask lumberyard personnel for help in selecting prime posts and boards.

To ensure a safe trip home from the building supply center, secure materials to your vehicle with rope or bungee cords. For large purchases, or if your vehicle cannot handle the load, pay a little extra and either have the materials delivered to your house or rent a truck. When you get home, store the lumber in a dry place off the ground until you are ready to use it.

Carefully choose nails and screws for the project. Zinc-coated nails and screws, or brass screws, are much less likely to rust or cause discolored streaks in wood than are uncoated nails. In general, use nails or screws that are three times as long as the thickness of the material you are fastening, but make sure the nail or screw does not come through on the backside. Never substitute nails for screws in any carpentry project. Screws make much more secure joints, particularly in projects that must withstand wind or any other type of movement.

A steady workbench is a tremendous help with carpentry projects, or you can recruit a helper to hold lumber while you cut or position it. Regard any type of saw with great respect, and always wear protective goggles when using power tools.

Before painting wood, apply a coat of sealant (which may be clear or white, depending on the product you choose). For outdoor projects, use exterior enamel paint or a combination sealant-stain. 🌸

HAVE ON HAND:

- Miter box
- Backsaw
- Piece of scrap-wood
- Braces or C-clamps
- Power drill and bits
- Phillips-style flathead screws
- Countersink bit

SPLIT-FREE DRILLING. *When using a power drill to fasten two pieces of wood, select Phillips-style flathead screws.*

Support the piece you are mitering on a scrap of slightly wider wood. The wood beneath allows the backsaw to make a clean cut.

Place the piece to be cut in the miter box and set the saw at the proper angle. If needed, use braces or C-clamps to hold wood while you cut.

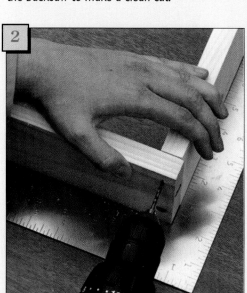

Set the pieces in place and drill a pilot hole through one piece into the other. Use a bit slightly smaller than the diameter of the screw.

Use a countersink bit to bore a space for the screwhead in the top board. Set the screw into the wood until the head is flush.

HERE'S HOW

CORRECT BLADE DEPTH

Before you cut anything with a circular saw, unplug the saw and check to see that the blade is set to about ¼ inch deeper than the thickness of the wood. This may seem like an inconvenience, especially if you are constantly switching between boards of different thickness. But here's why it's worth it: A saw blade that extends only slightly below the material will produce a much cleaner cut than a blade that extends far below the material. A blade set at the proper depth will also make the cutting process go smoothly. The deeper the blade is set, the more prone it is to binding in the wood and possibly causing the saw to buck or jump backward, jeopardizing both the project and your safety.

A Guide to Plants

Plants are an essential part of the landscape. They add color, texture, and interest. Plants also visually soften the edges of paved areas and structures, blending the components of the landscape into a pleasing whole.

There's great satisfaction in planting anything from an annual flower to a tree and watching it thrive. Keep in mind that even expert gardeners have plants that don't survive, so don't let a few failures discourage you.

Plants can be divided into three groups, based on their life span: annuals, perennials, and biennials. Annuals live just one growing season, usually sprouting from seed in early spring and dying at the first hard frost. In between they flower like crazy. Annuals are inexpensive, come in a wide range of colors and forms, and are easy to care for. Some common annuals that you may enjoy using include annual candytuft, ageratum, pot marigold, spider flower, marigolds, petunias, and cosmos.

Some plants, including snapdragons, wax begonias, coleus, and impatiens, are tender perennials grown as annuals. They are grown in the same manner as true annuals, but in warmer climates they often survive the winter and rebloom the following spring. Perennials come back year after year (although some have longer life spans than others). Plants like daylilies and hosta are herbaceous perennials; their stems remain soft and die back to the ground in winter. Trees and shrubs are perennials that have woody stems rather than soft herbaceous stems. While it's possible to grow perennials from seed, more often people buy plants that are at least a year old. Perennials usually bloom for a few weeks each year.

Biennials grow leaves the first year, flower the second year, then die. Because some reseed and continue to appear in the garden year after year, they seem like perennials. Sweet William and some species of foxglove and hollyhocks are biennials. Grow them from seed, or buy plants.

When deciding what to grow in your garden, consider the amount and duration of light your yard receives, how wet or dry the climate is, the type of soil, and how cold and hot the seasons are. Then match plants to those conditions. You can learn which plants do well in your area by observing other gardens and visiting local garden centers, as well as by consulting horticulture books. ❦

PICK THE RIGHT PLANT. *When you select plants, be sure each is hardy in your area and is adapted to the conditions in your yard.*

MULCHING. *Apply a 1- to 3-inch layer of buckwheat hulls, bark chips, or other fibrous mulch. Keep mulch about 3 inches from stem.*

DIG A PROPER HOLE. *Dig a hole as deep as the plant's container and twice as wide. Loosen but don't remove the soil in the bottom.*

PLANTING. *Remove the plant from the pot, loosening roots if needed. Place plant in hole, fill hole with soil, and gently firm soil around plant.*

FERTILIZING. *Apply slow-release fertilizer around plants to feed them for months. Use water-soluble products for immediate nutrients.*

WATERING. *Apply water slowly to soil at base of plant until ground is thoroughly wet. Avoid wetting foliage, which can promote plant diseases.*

HERE'S HOW

DIVIDING PERENNIALS

In just a few seasons, many popular perennials, such as iris and daylilies, can grow from small plants into large clumps. The larger the clump, the more crowded the plants become. Soon there isn't enough moisture, nutrients, and sunlight to go around. Symptoms of overcrowding include reduced flowering, pale green or thin leaves, reduced winter hardiness, and a dead spot in the center of the clump.

The best remedy for overcrowding is a technique called dividing. To divide perennials, use a garden fork to loosen soil around the perimeter of the clump. Slide the fork under a portion of the clump and lever it out of the ground.

Use a spade to cut the clump into smaller portions. Divide the smaller sections by gently pulling the plants apart with your hands. Each division can be one plant or many, but all should have healthy leaves, stems, and roots.

Plant divisions in the garden, spacing them to give them a few seasons growing room.

A Guide to Landscape Tools

PRUNING

Well-sharpened pruning tools make clean cuts in soft and woody branches. Match the tool to the branch size. Blade style can be bypass or anvil; bypass is more widely used.

PRUNING SHEARS

Hand-held pruning tools. Common designs include bypass, where the blades slip past each other like scissors, and anvil, where the cutting blade contacts a thicker bar. Ergonomically designed handles offer a comfortable grip while reducing hand fatigue.

LOPPERS

Loppers look like pruning shears mounted on a pair of long handles. The handles provide leverage to cut branches that pruning shears can't handle. Some models have a ratchet system to allow for cutting even larger branches.

DIGGING

Digging is heavy work, so select the right tool for each job and choose well-designed, high-quality tools to make hard work as easy as possible.

POSTHOLE DIGGER

Clamshell style has two hinged 12-inch blades on 44- or 48-inch handles. The blades cut into soil and hold it as it's withdrawn. The tool makes deep, narrow holes perfect for fence posts.

SPADE

A digging tool with a usually rectangular metal blade attached to a handle. The blade of a spade is often longer with a more shallow face than a shovel. Choose one with a foot tread at the top of the blade.

BUILDING

Building is a satisfying endeavor that demands the proper tools. Always wear appropriate safety equipment and follow manufacturer's instructions carefully.

CARPENTER'S LEVEL

A tool that indicates whether an object—or two points—is perfectly vertical or horizontal. Bubble levels use air and liquid encased in a tube; laser levels use a beam of light.

HAND SLEDGEHAMMER

Hammer with rectangular tempered steel head attached to wood or fiberglass handle. Weight of head varies from $2\frac{1}{2}$ to 5 pounds. Used to pound stakes, drive chisels, and tap mortared flagstones into place.

Special Tools

These tools are handy when you need them, but you may not use them very often. The more expensive tools, such as the compactor, you may choose to rent rather than purchase.

GAS COMPACTOR
Gas-powered tamping machine for preparing the base area for paths and patios. Metal plate stamps against the ground. Requires strength to control.

PRUNING SAW

Hand saw, usually with curved blade, used to prune branches. The saw teeth are set wide to inhibit binding when cutting and are designed to cut on the pull stroke rather than the push stroke.

POLE PRUNER (POLE SAW)

Pruning saw attached to a fixed-length or telescoping pole. Often a cutting tool with a mechanism similar to pruning shears is attached beneath the saw. Pole pruners can cut branches up to about 12 feet high.

SAFETY GLASSES

Wear protective eye gear when pruning, especially when cutting overhead branches. Glasses are available in flexible and rigid plastic. Choose a pair that protects the area to the sides of the eyes, as well as the front.

WHEELBARROW

Use for hauling soil and other materials and for mixing batches of mortar. Tubs are available in metal and plastic. Plastic is lighter, is easier to clean, and doesn't rust, but it can crack.

SPADING FORK

Versatile four-tined fork for digging, turning, and mixing soil and loose materials such as compost and straw. Requires less effort than a spade. Of the digging tools, one of the most gentle to the soil structure.

GARDEN RAKE

Stiff steel teeth on a straight or bowed metal comb attached to a long handle. Used to break up soil with the toothed side and to smooth it with the flat side.

MASON'S TROWEL

Flat, diamond, or rectangular blade attached to a handle. Used to apply mortar to flat surfaces and between paving stones or bricks.

GROUT FLOAT

Tool with rectangular wood or metal blade attached to a wood or metal handle. Used to level grout, plaster, or stucco.

COLD CHISEL

One-piece metal tool with broad blade and short, solid steel handle. Used with hand sledgehammer to score and cut brick and stone.

LAWN ROLLER
Metal or plastic drum attached to long handles, for tamping soil and firming seedbeds after planting. Fill with water or dry sand to desired weight.

POWER TILLER
A machine with metal tines powered by a gasoline engine designed to cultivate soil. Power tillers can be hand operated or self-propelled, with tines located in the front or rear of the machine.

Fashioning Outdoor Floors

Walkways and patios are the floors in the outdoor rooms of the landscape. And like any floor, they serve practical functions. Patios and terraces provide places to relax and entertain outdoors; if located near entryways, they also make it easier to find the door and to enter the house without tracking mud. Walkways and paths link the areas of the yard and can direct the eye to a focal point. Steps, which are a walkway that changes levels, offer an easier, safer way to negotiate a slope.

Outdoor floors can be ornamental as well as practical. Depending on the material, they can be formal or casual, elegant or earthy. You have a lot of choices, from hard materials such as bricks, which require subsurface preparation, to simple bark chips or gravel spread on the ground. Price varies as well, from costly flagstones to homemade stepping-stones. Each material has its own appeal and sets the mood for the rest of the landscape.

Whichever material you choose, plan your project well, and order enough in advance. And because these materials are heavy, give yourself plenty of time to move them to the site and install them. Make it easier for yourself by having these materials delivered as close as possible to the site where you will be using them. 🎔

Creating a Spacious Landing

A flagstone landing provides a practical yet welcoming transition from the yard to the house. Flagstone looks solid yet warm, and it gives any house, even a new one, a sense of permanence. Flagstone is suited to almost any house style, from traditional to modern, from a cottage to an estate.

Flagstone that's evenly thick and has straight edges is easiest to fit and make level. It's also the most expensive. You pay less for stones with irregular shapes and thicknesses (called "crazy" stones), but you will spend more time fitting and leveling them.

This flagstone landing is set in mortar. Mortar helps the stones resist heaving and shifting, which can be a problem with stones less than 18 inches square. It also makes the surface more level, so it's easier to walk on and more stable for outdoor furniture. Since water can't readily soak into mortared gaps between stones, it's critical that you grade the area so water runs away from the house.

When laying out the stones, work in small sections of about 1 square yard, then set the section in mortar before fitting the next section. Do not walk on the stones until the mortar has cured, about one week. ❧

MORTARED FLAGSTONE

To determine the amount of stone you need, multiply the length by the width of the patio in feet. Add 10 percent for cut stone and 20 percent for irregular stone.

HAVE ON HAND:

▶ String

▶ Stakes

▶ Spade

▶ Garden rake

▶ Lawn roller or gas-powered compactor

▶ Crushed stone

▶ Sharp sand

▶ Flagstone

▶ Mortar mix

▶ Mason's trowel

▶ Rubber mallet

▶ Carpenter's level

▶ Broom

▶ Hose with spray attachment

Use string and stakes to outline the landing. Place string close enough to the surface to guide you as you dig, but not so close that you cut it.

Excavate soil from area. For uniformly thick stone, remove 6 inches plus thickness of stone. For uneven thickness, remove 2 more inches.

Grade excavated area so water drains away from house. This also reduces puddling on the landing. Compact soil with roller or compactor.

Spread a 4-inch layer of crushed stone. Top with a 2- to 4-inch layer of sand. Smooth with the back of a rake.

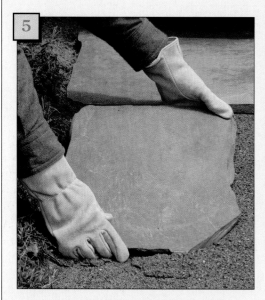

Water and compact the sand in one section. Plan the layout of the stones in that area, spacing them ½ to 1 inch apart.

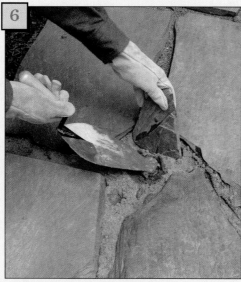

Mix the mortar. Lift a stone and use the trowel to apply mortar under it. Reposition stone in mortar; tap it into place with mallet.

Use a carpenter's level to make sure stones are level with one another. Continue fitting and mortaring stone a section at a time.

Sweep a 50-50 mixture of sand and dry mortar mix into spaces between stones. Hose down the area. Allow mortar to cure for 1 week.

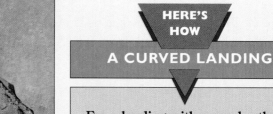

HERE'S HOW

A CURVED LANDING

For a landing with curved rather than straight sides, use a garden hose or heavy rope to outline the area, then mark the outline with flour or spray paint to guide you as you dig. Use "crazy" stone for this style of landing, because its irregular shape is easier to fit into curved lines.

Alternatives

TYPES OF FLAGSTONE

Flagstone is a catchall term for stone split into flat slabs that are at least an inch and a half thick. Flagstone is beautiful and long-lasting, but it's also one of the most expensive paving materials. Flagstone is most often used for walkways, steppingstones, and patios.

Depending on how the stone is cut, the edges can be irregular or straight, and the thickness can be uniform or variable. When choosing stone, consider the effect you want. A landing made of straight-edged stones looks more formal than one of irregularly shaped stone.

Some stones, such as limestone and some sandstones, are porous and can crack if they absorb water and then freeze (though they can be treated with a sealant that inhibits water absorption). Their strength depends on the pressure and moisture present when they formed. They have an open-grained texture, so they aren't slippery when wet and are a good choice for rainy, mild regions. Slate, bluestone, and basalt are strong, fine-grained, and nonporous. They can be slippery when wet.

SANDSTONE
Sandstone is sand held together by a natural cement such as silica or calcium carbonate. Colors include tan, pink, brown, blue, and black. Strength ranges from weak to strong.

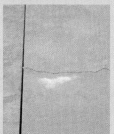

SLATE
Slate is fine-grained and dense, so it sheds water well. Slate comes in red, green, silver, gold, black, and mixed colors. It is durable and tends to split into evenly thick slabs.

BLUESTONE
Bluestone is a metamorphic sandstone that is both strong and water resistant. It comes in blue, green, gray, and brown. The most common type is Pennsylvania bluestone, which is one of the softer, smoother, finer-grained bluestones.

LIMESTONE
Limestone can be white, tan, gray, black, or striped. Its durability varies greatly, from weak to medium strong. The texture varies from smooth to pitted; it may have imprints of seashells.

GRANITE
Granite is a coarse-grained igneous rock containing large amounts of quartz and feldspars. These glassy minerals give granite its characteristic sparkle. Granite is very durable and comes in a wide range of colors.

Installing a New Brick Walkway

A brick walkway can be a dominant and appealing element of a landscape, one that both complements and is complemented by the plants that border it. Curving walkways, like the one pictured here, are especially inviting, as they lure the eye into hidden areas and combine solid material with a flowing form.

A well-constructed brick walkway provides a means of getting from one part of the yard to another for many years to come. The secret to a durable walk is the underlying base, so take time to make the base even and firm. Take special pains to make sure that the bricks are level, so they form a flat, even surface for a safe walkway.

This walkway is mortared, a method especially well suited to mild-winter regions where the ground doesn't shift as it freezes and thaws. The bricks in this path are widely spaced, giving the walkway an informal look. For a formal effect, space bricks closer together.

The bricks in this walkway are laid in an offset bond pattern. This means that the joints between bricks are staggered, so that no two line up with those in adjacent rows.

LAYING MORTARED BRICK

Make sure to select paving bricks, not facing bricks (the type used for building houses), which aren't as durable when in constant contact with soil. Depending on size, you'll need four or five bricks per square foot.

These instructions call for a water-filled roller to tamp the soil. For a smaller area, set a wide board on the ground and step on it heavily. For a larger area, consider renting a power compactor.

Before you begin have the utility company locate buried cables and pipes.

HAVE ON HAND:

- Garden hose or heavy rope
- Tape measure
- Trowel
- Flour
- Spade
- Shovel
- Garden rake
- Crushed stone
- Lawn roller
- Sharp sand
- Masonry mortar mix
- Masonry trowel
- Frost-resistant bricks
- Wooden spacer, 1 inch wide
- Rubber mallet
- Kneeling board

Outline the path with hose or heavy rope. Use a tape measure to ensure that walkway width is uniform. Sprinkle flour to mark edge of path.

Excavate area within outline to a depth of 7 inches plus thickness of brick. Use a flat-bladed spade to make clean cuts along edge of path.

Rake area smooth and spread a layer of crushed stone in center of path and along its length. Grade stone so water drains toward edge of path.

Tamp stone with roller and cover with a 2-inch layer of sand. Spread the sand uniformly, with the center the same depth as edges. Tamp the sand.

Mix the mortar. Working on a 3- or 4-foot-square area at a time, use a masonry trowel to spread a 1-inch layer of mortar on the sand.

Set bricks into mortar. Use a spacer to set them 1 inch apart on straight sections, closer on inside curves, and farther apart on outside curves.

Use a board to make sure running bricks are level. Bricks across the width of the path will follow the grade.

Tap each brick into the mortar with a rubber mallet. Use edge of masonry trowel to remove any excess mortar that rises between the bricks.

HERE'S HOW

CRUSHED STONE & SAND

To calculate the number of cubic feet of stone you will need, multiply the length of the walkway in feet times the width in feet times 0.33.

To calculate cubic feet of sand, multiply the length in feet times the width in feet times 0.17.

Alternatives

MIXING MATERIALS

There are a lot of good reasons for using more than one material when building a walkway. From a practical standpoint, you can use up materials left over from other projects. You can also save money by combining inexpensive materials with expensive ones. From an artistic point of view, you can create a unique landscape feature in which different shapes, textures, and colors interplay.

Common pathway materials include paving stones, flagstones, bricks, bark chips, and gravel. Limit the number of different materials to no more than three, combined in a simple, repeating pattern. The idea is to achieve variety by mixing textures, not a lot of different colors.

A quick method for building a pathway of mixed materials is to set steppingstones on top of bare soil, then surround them with gravel or mulch so that the surface of the stones is even with the surface of the surrounding material. With this method you don't have to prepare a sand base, as you would with a walkway of brick or paving stones. To prevent weeds from growing up through the mulch or gravel, cover the bare soil with landscape fabric before placing the stones. ❧

PATTERNED PATHWAY

You can also lay a garden path of unmortared brick for a more informal look. Lay your bricks in a pattern that suits you; patterns range from simple and geometric to more elaborate and ornamental, such as herringbone or basketweave. The pattern shown here is a modified basketweave. The amount of space you leave between bricks affects the tone of the design as well.

These bricks were laid with slight gaps, giving the path a relaxed feel, while still directing feet and eyes to the fountain focal point at its end. You can even omit some bricks from your path, filling gaps with topsoil and then planting creeping herbs or perennials.

You can lay a pathway like this on just a 1-inch sand bed. Before setting the brick, wet the sand using a fine spray, then drag a screed over the sand to level the surface. Tap each brick in place with a rubber mallet to settle it. Then sweep sand into gaps, and water to settle the sand.

For visual interest, line a dark brick path with pale-leafed plants, such as variegated hostas. Conversely, if the path is light-colored, for contrast grow a dark-leafed plant near it, such as a chocolate-leafed coral bells. ❧

A Path to a View

Decorative steppingstones make a charming path through the garden. When you make the stones yourself, the path becomes an expression of your creativity. Steppingstones are inexpensive and easy to make, so you can experiment as much as you like. They're a great project to do with children. They also make a thoughtful, one-of-a-kind gift for garden-loving friends.

Making stones requires just a few basic materials. First, you need a mold to hold the concrete in place as it dries. You can buy sturdy plastic molds designed for this purpose, either plain or with a relief pattern or a decorative shape. You can also make your own mold from household items such as metal cake or pie pans, sturdy cardboard gift or pizza boxes (reinforced with duct tape), or the plastic saucers sold to use under flowerpots. For the concrete, either mix your own from equal parts of sand and cement, or buy a mix from a hardware store. Unless you're using a mold with a relief pattern, you need materials for the decorative inlays, such as bits of tile, marbles, broken pottery, colored glass, seashells, or pebbles. ❧

MAKING STEPPINGSTONES

A 60-pound bag of concrete mix makes about six stones. When choosing the inlay, consider that rough-textured materials form a firmer bond with the concrete than smooth ones do. Also, if you'll be walking on the stones, use a decoration that doesn't get slippery when wet.

When you mix the concrete, it should be quite thick, like firm cottage cheese. If desired, add a concrete colorant. 🌿

HAVE ON HAND:

- ▶ Tarp
- ▶ Mold
- ▶ Sand
- ▶ Concrete
- ▶ Wheelbarrow
- ▶ Water
- ▶ Hoe
- ▶ Masonry trowel
- ▶ Decorative materials, such as polished stones
- ▶ Flat board
- ▶ Stiff brush (nonmetal bristles)
- ▶ Towel

Plan your design by making a model. Fill a mold with sand and arrange the stones in the pattern you want.

Combine equal parts of concrete and sand in a wheelbarrow. Add water gradually to make a stiff mixture.

Fill an empty mold with concrete. Using a masonry trowel, chop the concrete several times to remove air bubbles.

Once air bubbles are removed, use the trowel to smooth and level the entire surface.

Following the model prepared in Step 1, press the stones into the concrete so they are just below the surface.

When all the stones are in place, use a flat board to level the surface.

HERE'S HOW

LEAF IMPRESSIONS

Using leaves, you can create stepping-stones imprinted with faux fossils. Instead of pressing the leaves into the surface of the wet concrete, arrange them on the bottom of the empty mold. It's okay if some leaves extend up the sides. Pour in the concrete, let it dry, then gently pull off the leaves from the surface of the steppingstone. Let stubborn leaves remain in place; weather and foot traffic will quickly wear them off.

Let mold sit for about 3 days until concrete dries completely. Remove the steppingstone by twisting the corners of the mold as shown.

Use a stiff brush to smooth edges and remove excess concrete. Wash with a light spray of water and towel dry.

Alternatives

SHAPED STEPPINGSTONES

You can buy or make stepping-stones in interesting shapes or with decorative patterns. If you want to make your own, you can find molds through specialty suppliers; your best resources for locating them are craft stores, the Internet, and advertisements in hobby magazines (try those for stained-glass hobbyists if you'd like to set glass into your steppingstones).

Most molds are simple shapes, such as rectangles or circles, with raised patterns such as flowers and sun faces. If you cannot locate a mold in the desired shape, check the bakeware section of a kitchen supply store for a cake mold.

When you plan the path, consider whether you want to use shaped or patterned stones as an accent in just a few places or for the whole path. If the stones will get much foot traffic, choose a pattern flat enough to allow sure footing. For added stability and to keep the stones clean, lay them in a bed of sand that's about 4 inches deep. Slope the path slightly downward toward one side to encourage quick drainage. Surround the stones with a clean mulch, such as shredded bark or pea gravel. ✺

A SIMPLE PATH

One of the fastest, easiest ways to create an attractive path is to use concrete paving slabs. You can find many types in the garden department of home improvement stores; for fancier ones, check with a stone yard. Stone slabs come in a variety of shapes and in colors ranging from plain gray concrete through reds and browns. The surface can be smooth, textured, stamped with patterns, or embedded with stone aggregate.

The variety of paving slabs available allows you to be creative when designing your path. Try combining different styles, colors, or sizes. The material you surround the stones with adds to the effect. For example, surround aggregate-embedded pavers with river rock, or surround smooth pavers with a coarse material such as gravel.

This type of path is easy to install. Set paving slabs close enough so that you can walk on them with a natural stride. If you are using square stones, you'll need fewer if you arrange them diagonally like a row of diamonds. Fill in around the paving slabs with gravel or bark mulch, making it level with the top of the paving slab to ensure your footing if you step off the slab. ✺

Installing a Tile Entryway

An ordinary concrete patio, entryway, or walkway can be transformed into an attractive, inviting area in as little as one weekend with the simple addition of a veneer of tile. Tile provides a durable surface that will last for years if properly installed over a concrete base. Its beauty and appearance are unparalleled among surfacing materials.

Using tile outdoors was once restricted to warm climates where there is no freezing and thawing. But with advances in manufacturing, there are now types of tile that can be used in almost any climate. When choosing tile for paving, stick to unglazed tile. Because glazed tile becomes slippery and unsafe when wet, it is better reserved for decorative accents in edges, trim, walls, and surrounding raised beds.

If you have never installed tile, be sure to get the proper tools for the job. Most of them are so inexpensive it is just as easy to purchase them as to rent them. It may also be necessary to seal the tile after it is installed to protect it from the elements. Ask the dealer where you purchase the tile if it has been treated with a sealant at the factory. If it hasn't, apply a good-quality sealant to protect the tile from scratches and to keep it from absorbing moisture. ❦

LAYING CERAMIC TILE

This 9 x 22-foot entry patio offers a warm welcome to the house, as well as a place to relax and enjoy the garden. The patio tile shown here is to be set in mortar over a concrete base. ❧

HAVE ON HAND:

- Straightedge
- Hand sledge
- Chisel
- Patching concrete
- Stiff scrub brush
- Bucket of water
- Concrete cleaner or pressure washer
- Chalk line
- Two hundred 12 x 12-inch patio tiles
- Three 50-pound bags of thin-set mortar
- Notched trowel
- Plastic tile spacers
- Carpenter's level
- Pointed, diamond-shaped trowel
- Two 25-pound bags of latex grout
- Grout-color silicon caulk
- Caulking gun
- Rubber grout float
- Large sponge

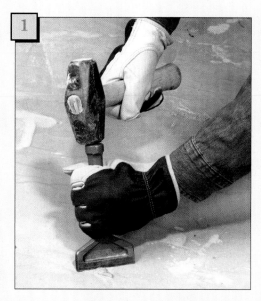

Use a straightedge to make sure concrete base is smooth. Chip away high spots with a sledge and chisel. Fill low spots with patching concrete.

Clean the slab with a stiff scrub brush and water. Use concrete cleaner for stubborn dirt, or rent a pressure washer. Allow surface to dry thoroughly.

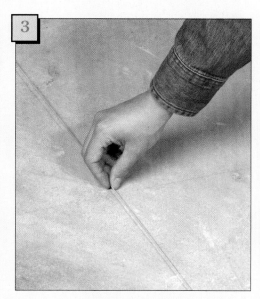

Mark center of patio by snapping a chalk line diagonally from opposite corners. Plan layout by laying several tiles here; don't mortar them.

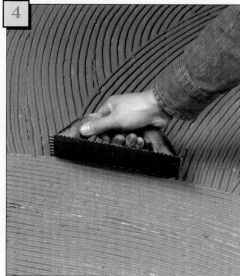

Spread a thin layer of mortar on a small section of the concrete with a masonry trowel. Use a notched trowel to create grooves in the mortar.

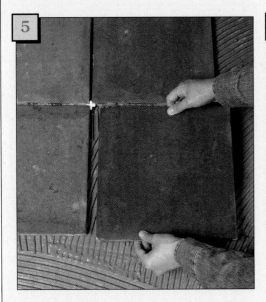

Use plastic spacers to keep tiles evenly spaced; remove spacers before the mortar sets. Check tiles with a carpenter's level as you work.

For expansion, at every 12 feet and where edges abut vertical surfaces, remove mortar from joint and replace with silicon caulk after mortar cures.

Allow mortar to set for 24 hours. Mix the grout and insert it into the crevices between the tiles with a rubber grout float held at a 45° angle.

Before the grout fully cures, use the rubber grout float to remove any excess grout. Wipe each tile with a damp sponge.

HERE'S HOW

DECORATIVE INLAY

Decorative tiles can be worked into any veneer pattern. Depending on the design and the size tiles you choose, you may have to cut tiles. For example, in order to incorporate the blue accent tiles seen in the photo on page 40, the corners of some of the larger terra-cotta colored tiles had to be trimmed. You can rent a power tile saw to make quick work of tile cutting. You can also cut tiles with a masonry blade attached to a circular saw. Score the line first with a glass cutter, clamp the tile in place, and then cut. Be sure to wear safety glasses, gloves, and ear protection when cutting.

Alternatives

TYPES OF TILE

The array of tile on the market is dizzying. There are hundreds of styles and colors to choose from to create the mood you desire in your outdoor living space. To get started on a tile facelift, first assess the space you're working with. Does it get a lot of natural light, or is it shaded? Light-colored tiles make an area seem more open and appear larger than it really is. Coordinate the color of the tile with your home to create a cohesive effect. Then measure and sketch the area in order to estimate how much tile you will need.

The most important thing to keep in mind when shopping for tile is to look for those specifically made for outdoor use. Look for the labels "vitreous" or "impervious." Select tile for walkways and patios that is unglazed or has a gritty finish to prevent slipping. Tile may vary from one brand to another and may even vary within the same brand. To ensure consistency in your project, be sure to buy all the tiles you need at one time, and preferably all from the same lot number. Personnel at specialty tile stores or home centers can help. Tile may be sold individually, by the square foot, or in boxed cartons. 🌿

QUARRY TILE
Quarry tiles are durable, heavy, and machine-made from dense clay. Their color varies from red to light tan, although some manufacturers offer a wider color range by adding color pigments to the clay.

SYNTHETIC STONE TILE
Synthetic stone tiles are made from clay and then stained to resemble stone surfaces such as sandstone or granite. They are a good choice if you prefer the look of natural materials, yet want the practicality of uniform size and shape.

TILE PAVERS
Tile pavers are bigger than regular tiles and are made to cover larger areas. They may be rustic, with the look of Mexican adobe, or more modern, with a regular pattern or an aggregate finish.

PATIO OR TERRA-COTTA TILE
Patio or terra-cotta tiles are made from ceramic materials that have been fired to provide a hardwearing surface. They come in earthy colors and have slightly irregular surfaces for a natural look.

CULTURED STONE
Cultured stone is a manufactured product made from Portland cement, natural aggregates, and iron oxide pigments. The finished product looks just like real stone and is often as little as half the price.

Terracing Safe Steps

Slopes pose special problems in the landscape because they are difficult to mow and awkward to walk on. In addition, unless they are covered with dense vegetation, such as grass, slopes are prone to erosion.

Rather than doing a lot of digging to alter the slope, an easier solution is to convert it to terraced steps. Besides making the different levels of the yard more easily accessible, steps make it clear to visitors where they should walk and eliminate the need for mowing. In addition, terraced steps give structure and add interest to the landscape, leading the eye to other levels of the yard.

The terraced steps in this project are easy to build because they are unpaved and require no special subflooring. Because the steps are not paved, they have the advantage of allowing water to percolate into the soil, alleviating possible drainage problems.

The steps are made with economical pressure-treated landscape timbers to stabilize the front of each stair, and gravel makes up the tread. If you wish, you can also edge the steps and pathway with timbers to create a barrier between the steps and adjacent plants. ❧

INSTALLING STEPS

These steps are made with what look like railroad ties. Real railroad ties are seldom used, however, because they contain creosote; pressure-treated timbers are used instead. Wear a mask when cutting to avoid inhaling the chemicals with which timbers are treated. ✿

HAVE ON HAND:

- Stakes
- Sledgehammer
- Post (about 4 feet tall)
- String
- Laser or string level
- Tape measure
- Spade
- Tamper
- Power saw
- Carpenter's level
- Landscape timbers
- Power drill and bit
- 12-inch metal spikes
- Landscape fabric
- Metal landscape fabric pins
- Crushed granite or marble chips

Hammer a stake into the ground at the top of the slope and a tall post into the ground at the bottom of the slope.

Tie a string to the stake at ground level. Tie the other end to the post so the string is level when checked with a laser or string level.

To determine how many timbers you need, measure the distance from ground to string at the post; divide by height of landscape timbers.

Use stakes and string to mark the side and front of each step. Use a tape measure to be sure the width of the steps is uniform.

Dig out the steps, making them as high as a landscape timber minus 1 inch. Fill low spots with additional soil. Tamp the soil firmly.

Use a power saw to cut the landscape timbers. Place a timber at the front of each tread. Check for level, and add or remove soil as needed.

HERE'S HOW

LANDSCAPE PINS

You can make your own metal pins for securing landscape fabric. Using wire cutters, snip the two curved ends from a wire clothing hanger to get pins about 6 inches long. To secure landscape fabric in place, push the ends of the pins through the fabric into the soil as far as they will go.

Predrill two downward-angled holes at each end of timbers. Hammer 12-inch spikes through holes into soil. Fill gaps behind timbers with soil.

Cover each tread with landscape fabric and secure with pins. Cover with decorative stone, such as crushed granite or marble chips.

Alternatives

SHADY NATURAL STEPS

By using slabs of native rock, you can make terraced steps look as though they occurred naturally, eons before humans arrived on the scene. In many regions of the country, you can harvest rocks on your own property, if you're willing to dig a few inches below the soil and use a pick-mattock or pry bar to loosen the rocks. You are likely to find many of the stones you need already in place or close to it, as you dig flat shelves along the slope while preparing the site. Or, instead of digging up stones, you can buy native stones from local stone yards, at a more reasonable price than flagstones brought in from other regions.

Plantings enhance the natural setting by softening the edges of the rocks and helping the steps blend into the surrounding landscape. Select plants that tolerate hot, dry conditions. A few good choices for tucking between the stones of a shady area are mother-of-thyme, Corsican mint, and woolly thyme, all of which tolerate light foot traffic. In addition, they give off a lovely fragrance when lightly bruised. On the edges, which don't get foot traffic, add low-growing flowering annuals such as impatiens and sweet alyssum. ❧

MORTARED FLAGSTONE STEPS

Steps of mortared flagstone create a stairway that is formal yet suited to a natural setting. For this staircase, choose stones that have been cut into flat slabs; they fit together more readily and form a flatter surface for sure footing. Choose a porous type of flagstone with a rough surface, so the steps don't become slick when wet.

To blend the steps into the landscape, plant perennials, ornamental grasses, and low shrubs on both sides. A stone path in a sunny location reflects the sun's light and heat, so choose plants adapted to bright light, fluctuating temperatures, and occasional drought. As a rule, such plants have small or thick leaves, often with a leathery or fuzzy surface. Prairie natives are a good choice. A few examples include the ornamental grass little blue stem and the yellow daisylike flower black-eyed Susan. Mediterranean plants, such as the herb rosemary, are also well adapted to bright, rocky areas. Herbs have the added benefit of releasing their fragrance when passersby brush against them. Plant large shrubs far enough from the path so that bulky support roots won't grow under the stones and push them out of place. ❧

Defining Boundaries

Fences and walls are perhaps the most versatile landscape element. If solid or nearly so, they make the yard private. They can screen unattractive views and call attention to appealing ones. If sturdy and tall, they enhance security by keeping intruders out and young children and pets in. At any height, they create a visual boundary that can serve as its own focal point or as a backdrop for plantings. You can even use fences and walls to divide a yard into smaller rooms, making inviting little nooks or separating living areas from utility and storage areas.

Your choices of fence styles and materials are almost endless, as a stroll through a neighborhood will prove. Wood, stone, brick, metal, and even plants can be arranged in dozens of ways to create attractive barriers. With so many options, you can build a fence that suits your tastes, budget, purpose, and willingness to maintain it.

Before building a fence, look into local ordinances and neighborhood covenants that specify the maximum height, setback from the property line, and allowed materials. In addition, if your fence requires posts set into the ground, before digging, contact your local utility company to locate buried cables and pipes.

Screening with Vertical Vines

Most yards have something to hide—a collection of garbage cans, an air conditioner, or the unattractive space under a porch. A good landscaping solution can turn a problem into an asset, such as this vine-clad lattice screen. It conceals the underside of a porch while adding color and texture to what was a dark, empty space.

The trellis also creates an opportunity to garden upward, a good solution for tight spaces. The lattice provides an attractive yet subtle backdrop for the vines, resulting in a combination that is handsome without being distracting.

And the trellis-vine partnership has a hidden benefit: The open lattice allows air to circulate, which helps to prevent plant diseases. In addition, it keeps moisture and odors from building up under the porch.

When choosing vines for the screen, consider whether you want to grow annual or perennial vines. Generally, annuals do not get as tall as perennials, nor do their stems become woody and heavy, but annuals do offer the opportunity to experiment with new species from year to year. If you prefer a perennial, select one that will not become too tall for its site nor too heavy for the lattice to support.

INSTALLING A TRELLIS

This lattice trellis is easy to build, as it uses the existing porch for support. Use premade lattice panels, which come in 2- and 4-foot widths.

Because a lattice panel flexes, it can be challenging to cut, so ask your lumberyard to cut it for you (be sure to have accurate measurements). If you cut it yourself, support the lattice panel on a workbench or on scrap lumber. 🌿

HAVE ON HAND:

- Tape measure
- Chalk or pencil
- Circular saw
- Bristle paint-brush
- Stain, paint, or sealant
- Four 2 x 4s, cut to size
- Power drill
- 3-inch galvanized wood screws
- Flowering vines
- Wood chips
- 1- and 1½-inch finish nails
- Premade 4 x 8-foot heavy-weight lattice panel, cut to size

Measure area to be screened and cut lattice panel to fit. Be sure perimeter of cut panel overlaps supports by at least 2 inches.

With bristle brush, apply paint or wood sealant to cut lattice panel. Treat both sides, especially the freshly cut surfaces.

To make the frame for the panel, use 1 x 2 lumber and cut four pieces to fit the sides and four pieces to fit the ends.

Nail side pieces to lattice, then nail end pieces, butting them against side pieces. Check to be sure the corners are square.

Turn the panel over and repeat Step 4, sandwiching the lattice between the 1 x 2 frames.

Predrill angled holes and use 3-inch galvanized wood screws to attach each lattice panel to support posts.

Plant flowering vines, such as Jackman clematis, at the base of the lattice. Spread wood chips on soil around plants to keep soil cool.

To train clematis upward when it first begins to climb, loosely attach growing tips to the lattice panel with twist ties.

HERE'S HOW

CLEMATIS CARE

Clematis, a gardener's favorite, will provide a long show of beautiful blossoms if you take a few simple steps to fulfill its special needs:

Keep roots cool. You can achieve this with a cool mulch of lawn clippings, wood chips, or similar material.

Keep lower stems shaded. To do this, be sure to plant clematis in a location that doesn't receive hot afternoon sun.

Increase alkalinity of soil. In acidic soils, mix a cupful of ground limestone into the soil when planting the vine to raise the pH.

Alternatives

VINES FOR A TRELLIS

By using the natural tendency of vines to climb, it's possible to grow beautiful flowers in tight places. Give them something to climb, and vines head skyward in search of sun, creating a sense of lushness despite a lack of ground space. Even in roomy gardens, vines can play an important role by creating a vertical line that balances the horizontal line of most plants. When densely planted, vines create a living wall that defines a space, blocks wind, and creates shade and privacy.

Vines vary in how much support they need. Perennial vines that grow to 20 feet or more often develop woody trunks too heavy for a simple support. Shorter or sparser perennial vines, such as some roses and clematis, are light enough for most supports. Annual vines, because their stems remain tender, are also a good choice.

When selecting vines, consider growing those that do double duty by producing edible fruit, such as squash, beans, and cucumbers. 🌿

SOUTH AFRICAN JASMINE
Jasminum angulare
10–20 feet
Zones 10–11
Vigorous twining vine with dark evergreen leaves and linen white, sweetly scented flowers from summer to fall. Fertile, well-drained soil; moderate moisture; full sun to partial shade.

BOUGAINVILLEA
Bougainvillea x buttiana
20–40 feet
Zones 9–11
Vigorous tender perennial climbing vine with evergreen leaves and brightly colored flower-like bracts from summer to fall. Fertile, well-drained soil; moderate to heavy moisture; full sun. Often sheds some leaves in winter.

VIOLET THUNBERGIA
Thunbergia batiscombii
6–10 feet
Zone 11
Fast-growing tender perennial vine with dark, grayish green leaves. Showy violet-blue flowers with yellow throats emerge throughout the year. Moist, well-drained soil; bright, indirect light. Prune in late winter to early spring.

VIRGINIA CREEPER
Parthenocissus quinquefolia
40–50 feet
Zones 4–9
Vigorous, woody, climbing vine with five-part medium green leaves turning bright red in fall. Inconspicuous greenish spring flowers followed by blue-black fruit. Full sun to shade; moderate moisture; average to fertile well-drained soil.

BLACK-EYED SUSAN VINE
Thunbergia alata
5–8 feet
Zone 11
Weak-stemmed tender perennial twining vine with evergreen leaves and yellow-orange, yellow, or white blossoms, most often with purple-brown central eye. Flowers appear from summer to fall. Full sun; well-drained, moist soil.

Installing a Privacy Fence

A privacy fence is one of the most solid boundaries, both visually and physically. It ensures privacy by providing a visual barrier between you and your neighbors. It also blocks noise, deters intruders, and prevents pets and young children from wandering off.

A privacy fence is a strong architectural element, one that can be too stark unless softened with decorative features. This fence is topped with a lattice panel that gives it an open, airy appearance. Other attractive options include a scalloped top, posts topped with decorative caps, and overlapping or alternating fence boards.

Plan your fence carefully. Sketch it to scale, noting how many posts you need and the spacing between posts: 8 feet is the recommended maximum. Ideally, posts should be evenly spaced, but uneven terrain can require that some sections (called bays) be narrower than others. Digging the post holes is the hardest part of installing a fence. If you have a dozen or fewer posts, a clamshell posthole digger is adequate. For more, consider renting a power auger, but be aware that controlling it requires strength. You can also hire a contractor to dig the holes, then finish the rest of the fence yourself.

WOODEN FENCE

These instructions are for one section of a 6-foot-tall fence using pre-assembled panels. Use pressure-treated lumber or a naturally rot-resistant wood. Seal or stain the completed fence. 🌸

HAVE ON HAND:

- Tape measure
- Stakes and string
- Posthole digger
- 0.5 cubic foot of gravel per post-hole
- Tamper
- One 8-foot 4 x 4-inch post per bay (first bay has 2 posts)
- Carpenter's level
- 2 x 4-inch boards for bracing
- One 50-pound bag concrete mix per 2 holes
- Power drill with screwdriver bit
- Galvanized flat-head wood screws

- Circular saw
- One preassembled 8 x 6-foot fence section per bay
- Paintbrush or power paint sprayer
- Exterior stain, sealant, or paint

Cutting List
- One heavy-duty 2 x 8-foot lattice panel per bay
- Four 8-foot 1 x 2-inch finished wood strips per bay
- Four 2-foot 1 x 2-inch finished wood strips per bay

Measure the locations of the corner, line, and end posts. Mark post locations with stakes, and run string between posts to mark fence line.

Use a posthole digger to make holes 12 inches wide and 30 inches deep. Add 6 inches of gravel; tamp firmly.

Set posts. Use level to be sure posts are plumb, and brace with two sections of scrap lumber. Check posts with level again and adjust.

Mix concrete in wheelbarrow. Add 2 inches of gravel to hole, tamp, and fill with concrete. Top of concrete must slope so water drains away.

Cure concrete for 24 hours. Affix fence to posts with wood screws. Use a carpenter's level to check for plumb before attaching.

Cut 2 x 8-foot pieces of lattice panel. On both sides of panels, use flathead wood screws to attach 1 x 2-inch wood strips to frame panels.

Use flathead galvanized wood screws to attach the framed lattice panel along the top of the preassembled fence section.

Apply exterior-grade stain, paint, or wood sealer to all exposed surfaces. Apply as many coats as is recommended on product label.

HERE'S HOW

INSTALLING POSTS

The strength and life of your structures depend on how well you prepare the posts. Choose the wood carefully. Avoid warped wood. Rot-resistant wood posts can be made to last even longer by soaking the bottom 24 inches in wood preservative overnight.

Another good way to prolong the life of a post is to coat the bottom end with wax, making it impervious to moisture and termites. Heat up the end with a propane torch. When it is very hot and begins smoldering, rub a candle against it until it is covered in wax.

To facilitate drainage in heavy soils or wet areas, place a stone or brick atop the gravel at the bottom of the posthole.

When backfilling the posthole, it is important to gradually add small amounts of soil, tamping down the area well with a 2 x 4, as the tamped soil helps secure the post in the ground.

Alternatives

FENCE STYLES

When you shop for fences, you will find a tremendous range of styles. The style you choose affects how much privacy you have. For the most privacy, choose a fence that's at least 6 feet tall and has fence boards closely spaced. If you don't need privacy but just want to direct foot traffic, establish a visual boundary, or create a backdrop for a garden, you have many options among shorter fences and fences with wider spaces between boards.

The style also affects how well air circulates. A solid fence blocks wind, which you might welcome if you live in a blustery area but dislike if you want to enjoy cooling summer breezes. Air circulation is also important for preventing some plant diseases, such as powdery mildew.

The choice of fencing materials can be intimidating. To make selection easier, choose a material that complements the style of fence you select and the style of your home and yard. For example, reed or bamboo enhances a privacy fence around a Japanese garden, and a fence of split rails adds a country look to any home.

STOCKADE
Fence boards are rounded slats (also called palings) with pointed tops. Excellent privacy. Wood usually left natural for a rustic look. Construction can be time-consuming. Materials available through lumberyards that specialize in fencing.

OVERLAPPING
Edges of boards overlap 1½ to 2 inches, making the surface three-dimensional. Time-consuming to build, but very strong, attractive, and private. Because boards overlap, no gaps form when wood ages.

PICKET
Boards are evenly spaced along the stringers. Not very private but allows good air circulation and is easy to build. Tops of boards available in a variety of shapes.

ALTERNATE BOARD
Fence boards alternate on either side of the stringer (the horizontal piece). Provides privacy but still allows some air circulation. Easy to build and attractive on both sides. Materials widely available.

WIRE MESH
Panels of 4- to 6-inch wire mesh are attached to posts. Provides physical but not visual barrier, unless used to support climbing plants. Inexpensive and easy to build. Wire comes in different gauges.

Installing a Garden Gate

An attractive gate can be much more than a doorway to your yard. A carefully chosen gate helps define the style of your landscape—the way you want your home or garden to feel from the moment someone sees it.

A gate is also a powerful element in landscape design. Any gate becomes a natural stopping point that divides two different scenes. For instance, it can distinguish the public street from the private property, the front yard from the back, or perhaps the garden from the rest of the landscape. The momentary pause at the gate should suggest in some small way what is to come. You can also use a gate to unify your landscape. Simply key the design and color of an entry gate to your front door or other prominent entryway feature, and the two elements become a visual link.

When choosing a gate that leads to a garden or other area of your landscape, you have a unique opportunity to add a custom touch that is both beautiful and functional. Equip any gate with a lock, and it can enhance your home's security while it keeps children and pets inside. ❦

FREESTANDING GATE

As a rule, a hinged gate should be no more than 4 feet wide to prevent it from sagging out of square. Choose heavy-duty hinges to ensure good support of the gate's weight. Attach hardware with screws that go as far as possible into the wood without coming through on the other side. ❧

HAVE ON HAND:

- Tape measure
- Pencil
- Stakes
- Two end posts
- Posthole digger
- Carpenter's level
- Shovel
- Two 50-pound bags concrete
- Wood gate
- 2 L-type gate hinges
- 1 gate latch
- Power drill
- Wood screws

- Screwdriver
- Nail
- Hammer
- String
- Line level
- Finial base and finial
- Handsaw
- Medium-grade sandpaper
- Damp cloth
- Stain/sealer for wood
- Paintbrush
- Scrap 2 x 4 supports

Measure gate. Use this measurement plus 1 inch to determine position of posts. Dig holes 2 feet deep and 1 foot wide.

Set the posts in the holes. Use a carpenter's level to be sure posts are plumb. Brace posts with 2 x 4 supports.

Mix concrete in a wheelbarrow. Fill the holes with concrete. Allow concrete to cure for 2 days.

On hinged side of gate, drill pilot holes for screws, and screw top hinge into gate frame. Install bottom hinge 6 inches or more from bottom.

Install latch on opposite side of gate from hinges. Drill pilot holes, then attach latch to gate frame with screws.

Mark locations for hinges and latch on posts. Loosely install mounting screws. Use level to check gate position before tightening screws.

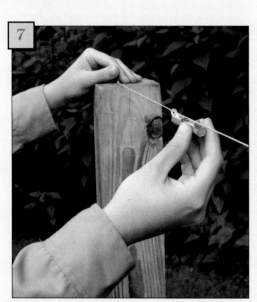

Measure desired height of one post; tap in a nail. Run string from nail to next post and level. Mark cutting lines and trim.

Attach finial base and finial. Apply two coats of paint to gate, posts, and finial.

HERE'S HOW

FINISHING TOUCHES

When your gate is completed, its simplicity and beauty allow it to stand alone as an attractive garden feature. Yet there are accents you can add that enhance your gate's function and appeal.

A strip of jingle bells attached to a decorative leather strap and hung near the gate latch cheerfully announce visitors as they enter the yard or garden. Be sure to look for bells that can remain outdoors and resist rusting. Many garden centers and specialty catalogs carry weather-resistant bells.

A narrow planting box can be attached to the inside upper horizontal gate support. Fill with potting soil and plant with cascading summer flowers. Remember that this narrow box will dry out more quickly than standard size window boxes, so water frequently.

Alternatives

GATEWAYS

A gateway is more than a gate. It combines two types of passageways, such as an archway and a swinging door. The archway makes the place of passage obvious, which is especially helpful if the gate is part of a long fence, is far from where visitors arrive, or is blocked from easy view. In addition, a sturdy archway provides support for climbing plants such as rose or clematis. The swinging gate serves the practical purpose of creating a barrier. The act of opening the gate gives guests a more concrete sense of transition between inside and outside than simply passing under an archway would.

The material the gateway is made from helps set the mood of the landscape. An ornate white trellis and picket gate are well suited to a cottage garden in the suburbs, while a rustic gate is ideal for a garden that features native plants or for a farmhouse-style home. The unpainted cedar gate shown here is easy to maintain, as cedar resists rot and weathers naturally from brown to a silvery gray. Planting a ground cover, such as hosta, along the base of the fence to which the gate is attached eliminates the problem of cutting grass along the fence. ❧

AN ARBOR PASSAGEWAY

A ready-made arbor is a quick, often inexpensive alternative to a gate. While it won't keep stray dogs out of your yard, it clearly signals to visitors where the entryway is and provides a place to grow climbing plants. You can find many different styles, from simple to elaborate. Garden centers usually carry several. For more choices, visit an outdoor furniture store, look in garden catalogs, or search the Web.

Ready-made arbors are available in metal, wood, and heavy-gauge plastic. Metal arbors have a classic, airy look. Because metal is malleable, metal arbors can have elaborate scrollwork not possible with wooden and plastic arbors. Over time, the finish on metal arbors can flake and rust.

Wooden arbors are usually made from a rot-resistant wood such as cypress or cedar. You can buy them painted or stained or finish them yourself. Popular shapes include flat-topped, arched, and pagoda-style. Many woods require regular upkeep to prevent peeling, fading, and decay.

Arbors made from heavy-gauge polyvinyl plastic resemble painted wood, especially from a distance. How authentic they look up close varies. Plastic's big advantages are lower price and low maintenance. ❧

Growing Living Screens

A group of closely planted shrubs is a living fence that provides privacy and security. It can also absorb noise and create a microclimate by blocking wind. A living screen can be a hedge of the same tree or shrub planted in a line or a staggered cluster of plants with different heights, colors, and textures. It can be pruned for a formal look or left natural and informal. In addition to shrubs, you can use vines, trained to climb on a support. Tall ornamental grasses also function as screens.

When choosing hedging plants, weigh the importance of the rate of growth and the mature height. Slow growers take longer to provide screening, but they require less pruning than fast growers.

A more visually interesting alternative to a hedge is a grouping of a number of different species of plants in a staggered arrangement. While a grouping like this is more natural looking, it does require more room. This type of planting offers several advantages over a single row: The screen will look fuller faster; you can space plants farther apart and thereby cut down on pruning; and if one plant dies, the screen won't have a gaping hole. ❦

PLANTING A SCREEN

This project combines evergreen shrubs and ornamental grass for a variety of shapes, colors, and textures. The feathery texture of an ornamental grass in the back and an interesting conifer in front of it complement the solidity of the evergreen holly and boxwood. The spacing for the plants takes into account their rate of growth as well as their mature size. This number of plants would fill an area about 14 feet long and 10 feet wide. 🌿

HAVE ON HAND:

- Tape measure
- Stakes and string
- Spade
- Landscape fabric
- Landscape fabric pins
- Scissors
- Garden knife
- Hose or watering can

- Mulch

Plants
- Switch grass
- Rhododendron
- 'China Girl' holly
- Western arborvitae
- Boxwood

Measure and mark the outline of the area you are planting. Clear sod, weeds, and other vegetation from the area.

Dig a hole for the switch grass in the center of the bed. Dig a hole for the rhododendron about 7 feet to the right of the grass.

For 'China Girl' holly, dig about 5 feet to the right and 4 feet in front of the grass. Place excavated soil in wheelbarrow.

Dig a hole for the arborvitae 5 feet in front of the grass. Dig a hole for the boxwood 4 feet to the left of rhododendron.

Lay landscape fabric over entire area; fasten with landscape fabric pins. Cut 2-foot-wide, X-shaped slits through fabric over the holes.

Remove a plant from its container and make a vertical cut in four equally spaced places about 1/8 of the way through the root mass.

Put the plant in its hole and fill hole halfway with soil. Water gently. Fill hole rest of way; tamp the soil gently.

Repeat Steps 6 and 7 for remaining plants. Slowly soak soil at base of plants with water. Cover the landscape fabric with bark mulch.

HERE'S HOW

CONTROLLING PLANT SIZE

Because the arborvitae, rhododendron, and holly can grow very large, prune them to keep their size in check. Make the base of the plant slightly wider than the top so sunlight reaches the whole plant. Cut the ornamental grass off about 1 foot from the ground before new growth begins in spring.

Alternatives

SCREENS FOR PLANTING

When choosing plants for a living screen, consider the amount of time during the year that the plants will have leaves. Evergreen conifers are widely used, but you can also grow broad-leafed evergreens or deciduous plants with interesting shapes. Ornamental grasses are becoming a popular choice, because they grow quickly and provide screening through the winter if you wait until spring to cut back the dead leaves. Ornamental grasses also have a texture and movement that complement more static shrubs.

Consider also the mature width of the plants. You can either space plants far enough apart that they won't be crowded when they mature or, if you want the screen to be dense when young, plant them close together and plan to remove some plants as they become crowded. Take into account the mature height, too. When possible, choose plants that don't get so tall that they require pruning to keep their size in check.

Finally, look at the rate of growth. A fast-growing plant fills in sooner. Mature width and height are less of a concern for very slow-growing plants, since it can take them a decade or more to reach full size. 🌺

JAPANESE WHITE PINE
Pinus parviflora
30–60 feet
Zones 5–9
Soft-textured tree with dark blue-green needles and informal habit. Small, decorative, reddish brown cones; salt tolerant; well-drained, average soil; full sun; moderate water; slow-growing dwarf varieties available.

CAROLINA ALLSPICE
Calycanthus floridus
8–10 feet
Zones 5–9
Bushy shrub with glossy, dark green leaves and maroon-brown, pineapple-scented late spring blossoms. Full sun in cool climates, afternoon shade in warmer regions. Well-drained, fertile soil; moderate moisture.

WESTERN ARBORVITAE
Thuja plicata
70–90 feet
Zones 5–9
Tall, conical evergreen tree with reddish, fissured bark. Full sun; deep, well-drained, moist soil. Many excellent smaller varieties available, including 'Atrovirens', 'Stribling', and 'Zebrina'.

GRAHAM THOMAS ENGLISH ROSE
Rosa 'Graham Thomas'
5–6 feet
Zones 5–9
Fast-growing rose with arching canes and abundant multipetaled, golden yellow, richly fragrant flowers in late spring. Full sun; well-drained soil amended with compost; average moisture. Looks best when planted in groups of three or more.

JAPANESE UMBRELLA PINE
Sciadopitys verticillata
30–40 feet
Zones 5–9
Slow-growing, conical evergreen tree with long, shiny, dark green needles. Full sun to partial shade; deep, well-drained soil; average moisture. Needles of some trees may turn bronze-green in winter.

Stacking a Low Stone Wall

A dry stone wall (also called dry stack) is held together by gravity, not mortar. The ancient stone walls that crisscross rural Europe and New England today are proof of the stability of this method of construction.

Because mortar doesn't bind the stones to one another, they are free to shift as needed as the ground below expands and contracts during winter's cycles of freezing and thawing.

You'll need three basic shapes of rock: flat, squarish, and regular for ends, corners, and the top of the wall; long stones equal to or greater than the width of the wall to tie the wall together across its width; and small, wedge-shaped stones to use as shims under larger stones and to fill gaps.

These instructions are for a wall against a bank. It's designed to be decorative, not a functional retaining wall. The wall should lean slightly against the bank for stability. Give it a 2- to 3-inch inward slope for each foot of height.

If you intend to grow plants in the gaps between the stones, plant them as you build the wall so you can firm the soil around the roots and water them thoroughly. For a more natural look, space plants at intermittent intervals.

DRY-LAID STONE

The building techniques described here will help create a stable wall. The wall has a wide, deep base, or footing, with stones that slope toward the bank, and stretcher stones that span two or three stones below them.

Figure on using 1 ton of stone for a wall approximately 30 cubic feet (for instance, 18 inches tall, 1 foot deep, and 20 feet long). 🌺

HAVE ON HAND:

▶ Shovel or spade

▶ Stakes and string

▶ Carpenter's level

▶ Stones

▶ Heavy gloves

▶ Soil for fill

▶ Hammer

▶ Line level

▶ Plants

▶ Trowel

▶ Potting mix

Excavate the footing, ⅔ as wide as wall is high. Run string at wall height around stakes placed at corners. Check with a level.

Place the first layer, or course, using the largest stones first.

Set the second course, placing center of upper stones over joint between stones beneath. Place this course about ¼ inch closer to bank.

Continue adding courses, placing each one about ¼ inch closer to bank than previous one. Place thinner edge of stones toward bank.

Fill any space between bank and wall with soil. For added stability, occasionally use a long stone that covers two or three smaller stones below.

Fill openings with small stones. Steady unbalanced stones by tapping in thin stones beneath them. Check each course with a line level.

Use large, flat stones for the final course. Set these snugly across entire course. Set plants in gaps between top stones; fill with potting mix.

For cascading plants, dig a hole in the bank just behind a top stone. Set the plant in the hole and fill around the roots with soil or potting mix.

HERE'S HOW

KNOW YOUR ROCKS

Traditionally, stone walls are made from local rock. Using readily available material is economical and ensures that the wall fits the natural landscape. You can find three cuts of stone: rubble is irregular, rounded stones, which are the hardest to fit together; evenly cut stone, called ashlar, is easiest to stack; roughly squared stones are a compromise—not as flat as ashlar but not as irregular as rubble.

Alternatives

PLANTS FOR ROCK WALLS

Alpine plants, which grow on mountains above the tree line, are ideal for rock walls, which mimic their natural habitat. Adapted to life in crevices between rocks, alpines are among the toughest plants you can grow. They tolerate wide temperature fluctuations, as surrounding rocks absorb heat during the day, then cool off drastically at night. They also tolerate soil that is usually shallow, infertile, and prone to drying. Alpines generally have long root systems that enable them to find water deep in the soil even when the soil surface is dry.

In addition to alpines, a number of other plants find growing in a rock wall quite to their liking. Plants such as hens and chicks require little care and spread through narrow crevices quickly. Other plants that can brighten up a stone wall include small spring bulbs, herbs, and strawberries. If you're not sure whether a plant you like can survive in a rock wall, consider these traits that many rock lovers share: wiry stems, sprawling or mounded habit, small size, small but abundant flowers, thick or hairy leaves, and grayish leaves. 🌸

SANDWORT
Arenaria spp.
2–3 inches
Zones 4–8
Very low-growing, vigorous ground cover with threadlike, bright green leaves and tiny white flowers in spring and summer. Full sun; poor, gravelly, well-drained soil; moderate watering. Can be invasive.

SEA PINK
Armeria maritima
4–6 inches
Zones 4–9
Clump-forming plant producing rounded mounds of narrow, dark green leaves beneath stiff stalks of bright pink flowers in spring and summer. Very well-drained, average soil; full sun; use gravel or stone mulch; salt tolerant.

CORSICAN MINT
Mentha requienii
½–1 inch tall
Zones 5–9
Very low-growing perennial with tiny, dark green, peppermint-scented leaves and small lilac flowers in summer. Shade or dappled sun; moist, well-drained soil amended with organic matter such as peat.

MAIDEN PINK
Dianthus deltoides **'Arctic Fire'**
4–6 inches
Zones 4–11
Low-growing perennial with short, grasslike, green leaves and small, brilliant magenta flowers in summer. Full sun; well-drained neutral to slightly alkaline soil; use stone or gravel mulch; avoid organic mulches.

HEATH
Erica cinerea **'Aurea'**
10–12 inches
Zones 5–7
Compact shrubs with needlelike, short, evergreen leaves and tiny, urn-shaped red, pink, or white flowers in summer to fall. Moist, well-drained, acidic soil; full sun; moderate moisture. Many varieties, such as 'Aurea', with golden foliage.

Creating Shade: Overhead Structures

On a summer day, a cool expanse of shade is a welcome oasis from the hot sun. Even when viewed from the air-conditioned indoors, shade is soothing to the eye. If you are fortunate enough to have a yard with natural shade from tall trees, you can preserve and enhance it by pruning shade trees properly. If your yard lacks shade, or you want more of it, you can build a shading structure, such as an arbor or a pergola, then use fabric or fast-growing vines to cover it. When building a shading structure, you can use a variety of materials, from wood to lightweight reinforced nylon. Depending on the materials you use, the effect can be rustic or elegant, classic or contemporary.

As you create shady spots, remember that whatever you put up will prevent light and water from getting to plants beneath the cover. Even if the covering is semipermeable, you may need to provide supplemental watering. Consider also whether the sides of the structure will block breezes. Unless you live in a windy area where you need a structure that can function as a windbreak as well as a source of shade, keep the structure open in the direction of prevailing summer breezes. 🌸

Using Natural Shade from Trees

Shade from trees is invaluable on a hot summer day, but shade does more than provide relief. A tree-shaded house requires less cooling in the summer, cutting air-conditioning costs. Plants growing under shade trees lose less water through their leaves than those in full sun, and so require less watering. And shade trees increase property values.

To create a shady canopy under which you can relax or entertain, you will need to do some thoughtful, well-planned pruning. Take a good look at the area where you would like to create your canopy and be sure there is a ceiling of branches with which you can work. When pruning mature trees, remove limbs that are dead, diseased, or damaged, as well as those that rub other limbs or form a weak angle with the trunk. Also remove branches too close to buildings or utility wires and those that block important lines of sight.

Remember these basic safety principles when pruning: Always wear eye protection. Only remove tree limbs that you can reach from the ground using a pruning or pole saw. Hire a licensed tree service to cut limbs that require a larger saw or climbing. Never use a chain saw to cut a limb above your head.

PRUNING A CANOPY

Pruning large branches requires a three-cut technique that prevents the weight of the branch from stripping bark. Pruning small branches calls for fewer steps but still demands attention to the location and angle of the cut.

The pruning tool you use depends on the diameter of the limb. Use a saw for limbs more than 2 inches thick, loppers for branches up to 2 inches thick, and hand pruners for branches up to ¾ inch thick. It's good practice to wear safety goggles whenever you're pruning, especially if you are working on branches over your head! Before you begin, make sure your tools are sharp. After pruning, don't paint the wound. Wound dressings can actually prevent healing.

These instructions do not apply to fruit trees, which require different pruning methods. ❦

HAVE ON HAND:

▶ Bow saw   ▶ Hand pruners

▶ Pruning saw   ▶ Safety goggles

▶ Loppers

Using a bow saw, set blade on underside of limb about a foot from the trunk. Saw upward a bit less than halfway through branch.

Place blade on top of limb. Saw through top of branch, 2 inches farther from trunk than the undercut, until branch breaks off from the tree.

To remove the remaining stub, make an upward cut just beyond collar, where branch attaches to tree. Cut less than halfway through branch.

Saw completely through the stub from the top until the stub falls away. Be sure not to cut the collar, as the collar will help heal the wound.

Remove small branches with a pruning saw or loppers. Cut branch just outside collar, leaving a short stub. Take care not to damage collar.

Remove branches that grow toward center of tree. Use hand pruners or loppers to cut small branches and a pruning saw for larger ones.

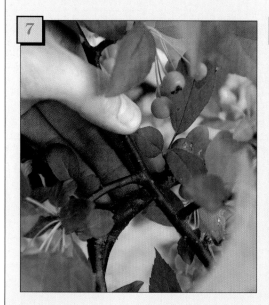

Branches that rub against each other can weaken the tree. Remove the branch growing toward the center or one that is unhealthy or damaged.

Midway through growing season, hang a few 1-pound weights on any young branch that grows at less than a 45° angle to the adjoining branch.

HERE'S HOW

WHEN TO PRUNE

Winter is the best time to prune deciduous trees—those that lose their leaves in autumn. Do not prune them in spring when they are growing new leaves, as the sap will bleed and can promote disease. Do not prune in autumn when leaves are falling and before tree goes dormant, as this can promote new growth that would be too tender to withstand the cold of winter.

Avoid pruning elms and oaks from late winter to early summer, when Dutch elm disease and oak wilt are most easily spread.

Prune spring-flowering trees and shrubs, such as dogwoods and flowering plum, just after flowers fade. Prune summer-flowering trees and shrubs before growth starts in the spring.

Remove dead branches at any time.

Alternatives

GREAT SHADE TREES

What makes a good shade tree? Perhaps the most obvious criterion is that it must grow tall enough to provide shade—at least 30 feet. It should be relatively fast growing yet long-lived, so that both you and your heirs can enjoy its shade. Tidiness is a consideration for trees close to buildings and paved areas; a good shade tree doesn't have messy fruit or drop branches easily. If you want to grow plants or even grass under it, avoid shade trees with very dense canopies or shallow roots.

Beyond those factors, choose a tree suited to your growing conditions. Some shade trees are adapted to dry soil, while others require more water. Shade trees differ in their tolerance for pollution and urban settings. Consider the tree's mature size. While many species stay small enough for an average lot, others may too quickly outgrow it.

The trees on this list are deciduous. That's an advantage in most regions, because deciduous trees allow winter sun to warm structures below them and spring sun to reach daffodils and other spring bulbs.

Shade trees can also be used to solve specific yard problems, such as poor drainage. An attractive river birch, red maple, or bald cypress planted in a wet spot will soak up excess water and keep the area drier. 🌿

LITTLELEAF LINDEN
Tilia cordata
50–70 feet
Zones 4–8
Handsome tree with round crown of small, deep green leaves. Small, greenish yellow, fragrant flowers dangle under leaves in late spring to early summer. Foliage turns yellow in fall. Full sun to partial shade; well-drained but moist soil.

RIVER BIRCH
Betula nigra **'Heritage'**
30–50 feet
Zones 4–9
Vigorous, often multitrunked tree with attractive, reddish brown exfoliating bark. Insect resistant and heat tolerant. Glossy green leaves turn yellow in fall. Full sun to dappled shade; moist but not soggy soil.

KATSURA TREE
Cercidiphyllum japonicum
50–70 feet
Zones 4–8
Fast-growing tree with wide crown and small, heart-shaped green leaves turning russet red in fall. Full sun to light shade; deep, well-drained, lightly acidic soil; moderate moisture. Protect from wind.

RED OAK
Quercus rubra
60–80 feet
Zones 5–9
Vigorous tree with glossy green leaves, large spreading crown, and dark fissured bark. Full sun to light shade; deep, well-drained, acidic soil; moderate moisture. Foliage turns reddish brown in fall.

YELLOWWOOD
Cladrastis lutea
30–40 feet
Zones 4–9
Medium-sized tree with green leaves turning yellow in fall and large hanging clusters of sweet-scented, white wisteria-like flowers in spring. Full sun; well-drained average soil; moderate moisture. Protect from wind. Prune if needed in winter.

Installing an Attached Arbor

Arbors are classic garden structures that have made a comeback as cottage gardens regain popularity. An open arbor can provide a passageway and transition to another part of your yard, while an arbor with a bench beneath it offers a nook for pausing to observe the garden. Both styles of arbors, when covered with climbing plants, give shelter from the sun. Attaching an arbor to a fence can be particularly effective, since the pairing provides a sense of continuity. Avoid placing an arbor in the middle of the yard without relating it to surrounding structures or gardens.

An arbor is attractive any time of year. It is eye catching in the winter, when it can give structure to the dormant landscape. It is especially appealing when draped with vines during the growing season. Although climbing roses are the quintessential arbor plant, other perennial vines can dress up an arbor, as can a fast-growing annual vine.

To ensure that the arbor will last for years, use a rot-resistant or pressure-treated wood. Anchor the arbor firmly in concrete footings. If the arbor is placed next to a fence, attach it to the fence at several points, using heavy-duty, rust-resistant hardware.

BUILDING A WOOD ARBOR

When marking the 2 x 12s for the cut line of your arch, connect the marks in a straight line for a pointed arbor or in a curve for an arched arbor. ✿

HAVE ON HAND:

- Four 4 x 4 x 8 posts
- Stakes
- Posthole digger
- Tape measure
- Crushed stone
- Tamper
- Carpenter's level
- Scrap lumber for bracing
- Concrete mix
- Two 2 x 12 x 8 boards
- Pencil
- Saber saw
- Pad or belt sander
- Medium-grit sandpaper
- Two 2 x 4 x 8s
- Power drill and bits
- 3-inch wood screws
- Two 4 x 4s
- 6-inch spikes
- Hammer
- Two 4 x 8 lattice sections
- Twelve 1 x 2 x 8 lumber
- 2-inch wood screws
- Drop cloth
- Exterior-grade paint or stain
- 3-inch bristle paintbrush
- Roses

Stake out corner posts for a 4 x 8-foot area. Make holes 30 inches deep; pour 6 inches of crushed stone into each. Tamp.

Use level to check posts for plumb, then brace with scrap lumber. Mix concrete and fill post-holes to 2 inches from top.

Mark center of each 2 x 12-inch board. Mark 6 inches from bottom at center. From bottom corners, measure 6 inches toward center and mark.

Connect marks to form lower cut line of arch, curving lines as shown in the photo. Mark parallel line, 6 inches wide. Cut along lines and sand.

Center 2 x 4s horizontally atop end posts, leaving 1¾ inches on outside for arch. Check level. Drill pilot holes; attach with 3-inch wood screws.

Measure and mark posts 6 inches above ground. Drill pilot holes through posts. Cut 4 x 4 to fit between posts and attach with 6-inch spikes.

Position arches on posts so they butt the 2 x 4 headers. Drill pilot holes through arches into headers and attach with 3-inch wood screws.

Frame 4 x 8-foot lattice sections on both sides with 1 x 2-inch lumber. Drill pilot holes and attach to posts with 3-inch wood screws.

Measure distance between arches for slats, and mark to position them evenly. Attach slats to arches with 2-inch wood screws.

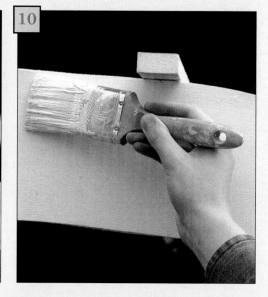

Apply two coats of an exterior-grade paint or stain. Allow to dry completely before planting roses at ends 1 foot from lattice.

Alternatives

ARTIFICIAL SHADE

When you need shade but there's no tall tree or climbing vine to provide it, you can create shade with a shade cloth. Traditionally, shade cloths were made from canvas or sailcloth. While canvas shades are still available, they can be hard to find. Today, most shade cloths are made from synthetic textiles that offer many advantages over canvas: They weigh less, fold more compactly, keep their shape even after being stretched, resist mildew and tearing, are easy to clean, block ultraviolet rays, repel water, and allow breezes to pass through so temperatures don't rise excessively under the cover.

Most ready-made shade cloths come with grommets installed in reinforced edges; you just thread a cord through the grommets and lash the cloth to an arbor, pergola, metal frame, or other structure. Shade cloths come in white as well as bright colors such as yellow and blue. To keep heat from building up under the cloth, choose a light color.

Synthetic shade cloths are available in a range of sizes through horticultural supply catalogs, as they are also used in the greenhouse industry. Companies that specialize in recreational and playground equipment also offer them. ❦

SHADE WITH CLIMBING ROSES

The charm of a rose-covered trellis is irresistible. Besides being colorful and fragrant, the climbing rose has a practical benefit: It casts shade. Because the long canes of climbing roses require some support, an arbor is ideal—especially one with many supports for training the canes.

Climbing roses have been around for generations and are becoming popular again, now that long-blooming, large-flowered cultivars with disease resistance are available. Roses that climb are divided into several classes. The most popular roses for arbors are ramblers, which grow quickly and have small flowers in dense clusters, and large-flowered climbers, which grow more slowly but have larger flowers.

Ramblers bloom best on new canes, so cut off a third of the old canes at the ground in the summer, after they finish blooming. Tie new shoots to the arbor with strips of pantyhose. For best blooms, train the shoots to horizontal supports. Wait until large-flowered climbers are several years old before pruning, because they bloom on old wood. When the plant reaches the height you want, you can prune during the dormant season. As with ramblers, tie new shoots to the arbor. ❦

A Vine-Covered Pergola

A pergola is an arborlike structure of columns or posts that support an open roof of cross-rafters, over which vines or plants may be trained to create a cool, shady bower.

An attractive yet simple structure like this pergola is a focal point of the garden, leading the eye to it, then beyond it. Because a pergola has an open roof and sides, light, air, and water can pass through it. It can be large enough to cover a patio or smaller like this one, which invites visitors to wander through it to the garden beyond.

While a pergola is an eye-catching feature in any season, it is at its best in summer, when it offers support for climbing plants. Those plants, in turn, create inviting shade beneath it. In winter, a pergola can add interest.

Perennials, such as roses, are often grown beside pergolas because they come back year after year. If you prefer experimenting, consider growing annual vines, which give you a chance to try something different each year. If your pergola is large enough, you can enjoy each by growing both types, one on either side. 🌿

BUILDING A WOOD PERGOLA

These instructions are for a pergola that is 7 feet high, 6 feet wide, and 6 feet deep. For ease of construction, build the sides first, before setting the posts. Although these posts are set in gravel and soil, you may choose to fill the post-holes with concrete. ❧

HAVE ON HAND:

- ▶ Tape measure
- ▶ Pencil
- ▶ Framing square
- ▶ Four 10-foot 4 x 4 posts
- ▶ Six 68-inch 2 x 4 side rails
- ▶ Wood screws
- ▶ Power drill and bits
- ▶ Posthole digger
- ▶ 4 cubic feet of gravel or crushed stone
- ▶ Shovel

- ▶ Tamper
- ▶ Carpenter's level
- ▶ Scrap lumber
- ▶ Miter box and saw
- ▶ Four 8-foot 2 x 10 top cross-pieces, ends mitered at 30°
- ▶ Four 30-inch 2 x 4 angle braces, one end mitered at 45°
- ▶ Six 7-foot 2 x 4 rafters

Lay posts on a flat surface side by side, ends even. Measuring from top, draw lines across all four at 30 inches, 48 inches, and 66 inches.

On each pair of posts, toenail side rails with wood screws at each of the three marks to form two ladderlike side sections with three rails.

Measure locations for four postholes. Dig holes, 30 inches deep and 12 inches wide, spacing so side sections are 6 feet apart at post centers.

Add 6 inches of gravel or stone to holes; tamp. Place post sections in holes. Use level to check posts and rails, then brace with scrap lumber.

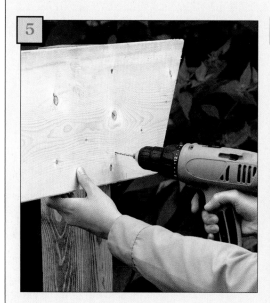

5

Fill holes, alternating 3-inch layers of soil and gravel. Make angled cuts at ends of 2 x 10s. Attach to top fronts of posts with wood screws.

6

Attach each angle brace to an upright so inside angle is 45°. Use wood screws to attach the other end to the back of the top crosspiece.

7

Lay a 2 x 4 rafter across the 2 x 10 top crosspieces, 8 inches from end, with 2-inch side down. Allow ends to extend evenly over sides.

8

Place another rafter 8 inches from other end. Space remaining rafters evenly. Fasten all rafters with wood screws.

HERE'S HOW

CHOOSING THE SITE

Because a pergola is such a dominant landscape feature, give some thought to its placement. It should fit into the area that surrounds it. If you have trouble visualizing the final effect, create a makeshift pergola in the place you're considering. Insert four poles (such as the metal poles used to hold wire fencing) into the ground where you are thinking of placing the pergola. Tie rope across the top to simulate the roof. Then view it from every angle, noticing both the way it fits into the site and what view it frames.

Alternatives

PLANTS FOR OVERHEAD SHADE

A pergola can be the centerpiece of the garden, but it stills needs the right vines climbing over it to project just the right mood. For example, an Old World ambiance is easy to achieve by growing grapes. The distinctive leafy foliage and clusters of hanging fruit turn your backyard into the summer garden of a Mediterranean villa.

Or your pergola could host the climbing canes of an antique rose such as 'Souvenir de la Malmaison'. What could be more romantic than sitting beneath a cascade of these rich pink blossoms, their perfume scenting the air.

When choosing vines to cloak a pergola, consider whether they have any traits that could make a stroll through the pergola less appealing. For example, although bees are an important beneficial insect, many people would be wary of pausing under a vine that's buzzing with them. Some vines are messy, dropping leaves and fruit. Others, such as cucumbers, are prickly. Aggressive, heavy vines such as wisteria can weaken a pergola.

Some vines are good climbers because they have tendrils or other means of attaching themselves to a support. Others tend to lean or sprawl more than climb; these you'll have to prop against the pergola, or gently tie in place. 🌿

CLIMBING HYDRANGEA
Hydrangea petiolaris
30–50 feet
Zones 4–9
Woody vine with stout, strong stems covered with peeling, cinnamon colored bark. Heart-shaped green leaves; flat-topped clusters of white flowers in spring. Full sun to partial shade; well-drained, organic soil; even, moderate moisture.

SOUVENIR DE LA MALMAISON CLIMBING ROSE
Rosa 'Souvenir de la Malmaison'
10–12 feet
Zones 5–9
Antique climbing rose with strong canes and large many-petaled fragrant blush pink blossoms in late spring. Full sun; well-drained, fertile soil; average moisture. Fertilize after flowering; prune when dormant.

BOSTON IVY
Parthenocissus tricuspidata
40–70 feet
Zones 4–8
Vigorous deciduous climbing vine with dark green mapleleaf-shaped foliage turning crimson to maroon in fall. Full sun to shade; well-drained average soil; moderate moisture. Many varieties; best fall color when grown in full sun.

CORAL HONEYSUCKLE
Lonicera sempervirens
10–12 feet
Zones 4–9
Woody twining vine with dark green leaves and tubular scarlet or yellow flowers in late spring to late summer. Full sun to partial shade; rich, well-drained soil; even moisture. Blossoms attract hummingbirds.

CHILEAN JASMINE
Mandevillea laxa
10–15 feet
Zones 10–11
Vigorous twining vine with elongated heart-shaped dark green leaves. Tubular white strongly fragrant flowers appear from summer to fall. Full sun with afternoon shade; moist, well-drained soil.

Ready for Recreation

One of the greatest benefits of a yard is having a place to play, entertain, and just relax. And a great lawn is fundamental to outdoor recreation. It provides a soft, cool, and attractive surface for family and guests to sit, mingle, or toss a football. If your lawn sees a lot of activity, choose a species and variety of grass that tolerates heavy foot traffic.

Having an outdoor play space is especially important for children. The ideal play area is fun and safe and fits with the rest of the landscape. The huge selection of play equipment available today makes it easy to build a playground that encourages active, imaginative play.

A playhouse is a uniquely magical play area, full of opportunity for make-believe. It doesn't have to be high off the ground to give children a sense of being on an adventure. By building it correctly, you ensure its long life as well as the safety of the children who play in it.

For adults, few features promote relaxation more than a hammock. Rather than screw holes into a tree, which leaves an opening for disease organisms, use rope to tie it around the tree instead. And remove the hammock at the end of the season to prevent girdling the tree. ❧

Creating a Children's Playground

If your yard includes play areas for children, you need not resign yourself to living with a structure that's out of place with the rest of your landscape. Instead, you can have a playscape that blends in with the rest of the landscape and still appeals to children.

The selection of play equipment on the market is nearly endless, so you can choose equipment that complements your house and landscape. For a contemporary house, for example, you might choose equipment made of colorful metal and other materials, while for a more rustic house, you could opt for wood. Evaluate also the ease of assembly and maintenance. If your children are young, look into sets of equipment that can be expanded as they grow.

Integrating the play space into your yard and garden needn't be difficult. While safety is the first consideration when choosing cushioning materials, you can select a material that suits the landscape, such as wood chips in a natural setting, or rubber crumbs for a garden with architectural or fanciful elements. Plantings around the perimeter create a visual transition from play area to garden area. Just be sure the plants are durable and not in spots kids use to enter and leave the play area. ✿

PREPARING A PLAYGROUND SITE

What cushioning material you use and how deep it is depend on the height of the equipment. The best shock absorbers are crumbs of recycled rubber tires, pea gravel, and bark chips, followed by fine gravel, then sand. In most cases, for equipment no more than 5 feet high (including the highest point of a swing's arc), 6 inches of any of these materials is adequate. For taller equipment, 9 inches of the most shock-absorbing material is recommended. ❦

HAVE ON HAND:

- ▶ Bow saw or pruning saw
- ▶ Lawn mower
- ▶ Landscape fabric and pins
- ▶ Landscape timbers
- ▶ Power drill and bits
- ▶ Hammer
- ▶ Spikes
- ▶ Rubber garden hose
- ▶ Utility knife
- ▶ Roofing nails
- ▶ Play equipment
- ▶ Ratchet or socket wrench
- ▶ Sandpaper
- ▶ Sand
- ▶ Garden rake
- ▶ Shredded bark or bark chip mulch

Remove hazardous overhanging branches from nearby trees. Use a bow saw for large limbs and loppers or a pruning saw for smaller ones.

Mow the area completely and cover with landscape fabric. Smooth out any wrinkles and secure the cloth with landscape cloth pins.

Set landscape timbers around the perimeter. Choose material treated with nontoxic wood preservative or use rot-resistant wood.

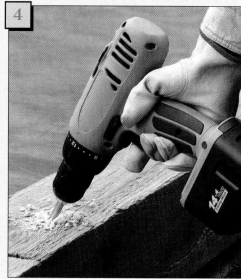

Drill a large hole through each end of timber at a downward angle, then hammer spikes through the hole and into the soil to anchor the timbers.

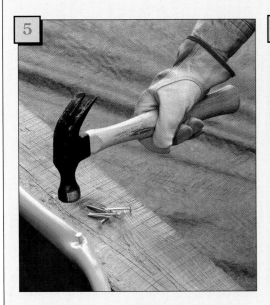

Cut a rubber garden hose lengthwise and as long as the landscape timbers. Cover the edge of the timber with the hose and nail in place.

Install play equipment carefully, following manufacturer's directions. Tighten connectors, smooth edges, and anchor equipment firmly to ground.

Spread a 3-inch layer of clean sand around play area and rake it smooth. Be sure the sand is clean and does not contain any pollutants.

Top with a 3- to 6-inch layer of shredded bark mulch or bark chip mulch. Grade so mulch is piled more thickly beneath play equipment.

HERE'S HOW

BUILDING FOR SAFETY

Play equipment is fun and gives children a chance to be active. To help keep children safe while they play, follow these guidelines:

- Always supervise children at play.
- Install guardrails on equipment that's elevated.
- Be sure all openings are either smaller than 3½ inches or larger than 9 inches.
- Space pieces of equipment at least 6 feet away from each other.
- Countersink all nails and screws.
- Provide shade for equipment that gets hot in the sun, such as slides.

Alternatives

ROMANTIC GARDEN SWINGS

A play area can be decorative as well as functional. Hanging simple swings from a bower in a garden sets a mood that is both romantic and nostalgic.

Swings appeal to adults as well as children, so the set's framework should be strong enough to support several hundred pounds. A simple metal A-frame swing set works well. For safety, set the feet of the frame in concrete. To blend the framework into the garden, cover it with dense, fast-growing vines. Good choices include morning glory, black-eyed Susan vine, and clematis.

If you want a more old-fashioned look than plastic swings on metal chains, make your own using strong nylon rope for supports and smooth boards for seats. If children will use the swings, it's safer to use plastic seats, which are harder to slip from, and strong metal chains. Cover chains with a plastic tube to prevent pinched fingers.

A soft floor of mulch beneath swings not only provides a safety cushion but also eliminates the need to mow. A thick layer of bark chips or another natural-looking mulch, such as cocoa hulls, fits the garden setting. 🌸

A SECRET FORT

A children's play area up in the trees, secreted away from the adults, can become a treasured childhood space for creative play, long remembered and appreciated. A fort such as this one offers kids a feeling of privacy and mystery. That sense is heightened when the fort is elevated above the ground—even just a few feet.

Siting the fort behind tall shrubs provides camouflage and adds the illusion that the fort skims the top of the canopy—without actually creating the hazard of extreme height. It also gives kids the chance to observe birds and squirrels from a new vantage point. For safety, build a fort near shrubs that are free from thorns. In addition, avoid plants that attract bees.

A fort can be simple enough that kids can help with its design and construction. You can use sturdy shipping pallets for the sides, being sure to sand them smooth first and hammer in any protruding nails. Attach the sides securely to a sturdy base. Add a canvas roof to your fort; it not only protects the fort's inhabitants but also prolongs the life of the structure by keeping water off the wood. 🌸

Growing a Great Lawn

A healthy green lawn is soothing to the eye, but its benefits go beyond beauty. Because grass, like other plants, gives off water vapor, it has a cooling effect in the summer. Turf also provides a cushioned surface for sports and is very effective for holding soil in place.

Different species of grass are best adapted to different regions of North America. Cool-season grasses, such as Kentucky bluegrass, perennial rye, and several species of fescue, are ideal for northern areas. In the South, grow warm-season species such as St. Augustine, zoysia, and Hybrid Bermuda grass. Lawns often struggle in transitional regions that are too warm for northern species and too cold for southern ones. Your local plant experts can guide you in choosing the species and variety best for your area. Besides climate, consider how much sun the lawn gets, as some species tolerate shade better than others.

These instructions are for installing sod, which comes in carpetlike sections of lawn grass about 2 feet wide and 3 or more feet long. Using sod gives faster results and is easier than starting from seed, although it is more expensive than seeding your lawn. Buy sod from a reputable supplier to ensure that the grass is free from insect pests and weeds. 🌼

PLANTING A LAWN

The best time of year to install sod is in the spring or early fall, so the roots can become established before the temperatures become extreme. A couple of weeks before you intend to plant, call your local supplier to be sure they'll have enough sod when you need it. Don't take delivery of sod more than a day or two in advance of when you plan to lay it, or it will dry out.

It is helpful to start laying sod against a fence or other structure to make it easier to keep each row straight. ❀

HAVE ON HAND:

- ▶ Spreader
- ▶ Lime or fertilizer
- ▶ Shovel
- ▶ Fine sand
- ▶ Stones, pavers, or bricks
- ▶ Power tiller
- ▶ Garden rake
- ▶ Water-filled roller
- ▶ Lawn sprinkler
- ▶ Sod
- ▶ Kneeling board
- ▶ Grass rake

Hire a professional to do any major grading or drainage work. Test soil and add any lime, fertilizer, and other soil amendments as needed.

To install a mow strip along beds and fences, dig a 3-inch trench and line it with 2 inches of fine sand. Lay stones, pavers, or bricks on top.

Remove all weeds and rocks. Use a power tiller to loosen soil. Rake the area until smooth, breaking up any large clumps of soil.

Firm the soil, using a roller filled with about 25 gallons of water (about 200 lbs.). Moisten, but don't soak, the soil to a depth of 6 inches.

Carry a rolled-up length of sod to lawn site, and unroll it onto the soil. As you work, place section edges snugly together without overlapping them.

Kneel on a board on the first course of sod. Roll out second course a section at a time. Align center of each piece with seam in the row before it.

Use a roller, filled with about 25 gallons of water, to press and smooth the sod into place. Rake the lawn thoroughly with a metal or bamboo rake.

Water the lawn deeply when job is completed. Until the grass is established, water once a day in cloudy weather; twice a day if sunny.

HERE'S HOW

BARING THE SOIL

Use one of the following methods for removing existing grass and weeds before you start your new lawn.
- Cover the area with black plastic during the summer. Leave the ground covered for 8 to 12 weeks.
- Power till the area. Allow 2 to 3 weeks for regrowth, then till again. Repeat one more time.

Alternatives

A DECK FOR ENTERTAINING

A well-designed deck is a perfect spot for dining, entertaining, and relaxing.

The deck should be large enough to accommodate your family and the number of guests you usually entertain. A 10- by 10-foot deck, for example, seats six people. Build the railings strong enough to support the weight of anyone leaning or sitting on them. Or, better yet, build in seating around the edges of the deck. For an easy-to-clean deck, space floorboards wide enough for dirt to fall through, space the bottom railings high enough that you can sweep dirt under them and off the deck, and locate it close to an outdoor faucet so you can hose it off.

If you live in a region with hot summers, be sure the deck is shaded in the afternoon.

When evaluating building materials, weigh cost and maintenance. Pressure-treated pine or fir is the least expensive but requires regular maintenance. Naturally rot-resistant cypress and cedar also require maintenance and are expensive. A third choice is wood polymers, which are waste wood fibers mixed with recycled plastic. These resemble wood and, though as expensive as a premium wood, require almost no maintenance. 🌼

SUITING THE SITE

Some site conditions make it nearly impossible to grow a grass lawn. A location can be too shady or too dry, or the soil might be too sandy, acidic, or alkaline. Some people go to great trouble and expense to modify those conditions, with varying success. Rather than fighting the site, it's much more sensible to make the most of what it offers.

One approach is to grow plants better adapted to the conditions that exist. For example, in a shady site, grow a shade-loving ground cover. By choosing one with light-colored variegation, you can make the area seem lighter. If the ground is acidic and shady, encourage moss to grow there. One simple way is to use an old blender to mix a small amount of moss with buttermilk and spread it on the ground. In sandy soil, such as those found along the coast, grow native grasses and wildflowers.

Another way to deal with a lawnless site is to cover areas that would normally be lawn with a stone or bark mulch, so you can still walk and place outdoor furniture on the site, just as you would if there were a lawn. Then surround the area with attractive plants in containers or raised beds filled with good soil. 🌼

Making an Outdoor Grilling Nook

As summer heats up, most cooks want to escape the hot kitchen and head to a cooler venue outside. A grilling nook can make preparing alfresco meals so simple and pleasurable, you may not want to return to the kitchen until cold weather arrives.

In designing an outdoor grilling nook, consider how you will use it. Make the path from the kitchen to the nook short and easy to navigate, so shuttling food items back and forth will be uncomplicated. Consider the design of your house, and choose materials for the grilling nook that will complement existing structures so the nook fits into the landscape seamlessly. For instance, if your home has a stone façade, choose stone of the same color for the grilling nook. Situate your nook so it is protected from the sun and, especially, the wind. Your house, hedges, or fences can help to divert the wind and provide late afternoon shade for the barbecue chef.

Also take into account where the meal will be enjoyed and, on average, how many people will be eating at any given time. Site the grilling nook to allow enough space for a dining area that will not be cramped. ❧

BUILDING A GRILLING SPACE

This 5½ x 5½-foot outdoor grilling nook is constructed from flat stone, which is much easier to stack and fit than rounded boulders. There is no mortar used in the construction, which makes building go quickly and easily. The broad top surface of the stone wall is covered with attractive slate to provide the perfect place for staging a meal. There's ample space to hold items to be grilled, grilling utensils, and food hot off the fire. 🌿

For the foundation, mark an area 5½ by 5½ feet with wooden stakes. Dig out the foundation to a depth of 1 foot.

Fill the excavated foundation area with a 4-inch layer of crushed stone. Check area with a level.

Lay stones for the foundation using the largest stones first. Position each stone to get the best fit. Fill gaps with small stones.

Lay another layer, staggering stones to overlap those below so joints between stones do not line up.

Continue until foundation is 1 foot high, checking each layer for level. Mark grill nook, centered, 2 feet wide and 2 feet deep.

To form a support 6 inches above the foundation for the grate, extend one layer of stones about 2 inches into the grilling area.

Form a support 24 inches above the foundation for the grill, following directions in Step 6.

Fit flat stones across the top of the grilling nook. Wedge small stones underneath the larger ones to firm and level the top layer of stones.

HERE'S HOW

MAKE A SLOPE GUIDE

To make a stable stone wall built without mortar, each course of stone must be somewhat more narrow than the course below it. This creates walls with faces that slope inward ever so slightly. Help keep the slope of the wall consistent by making a guide to use as you lay each course of stone. Use one nail to fasten a 2-foot 1 x 4 to a 4-foot 1 x 4 to form an "L." Tilt the longer board in toward the shorter board to form the angle of the setback. Nail a brace between the two boards to hold them at that angle. Then simply hold your guide up against the wall with the long board against the face of the wall and the short board level to check the slope as you go.

Alternatives

BUILT-IN GRILL

A grilling nook can offer many of the amenities of a well-appointed kitchen if you choose to go with a built-in grill. The menu will not be limited to hamburgers and steaks with specialty grills. Some offer built-in smokers—pullout drawers that hold wood chips to impart a particular flavor to grilled foods. Others offer rotisseries or burners for cooking with pots.

Installing a built-in grill such as the one shown in the photo requires outdoor electrical cable, a natural gas line, and water if a sink is added. These can be routed to the site underground or via an exterior wall if the grilling nook is near the house. If you live in a cold climate, be sure the water pipes are set below the frost line. Natural gas lines should be buried at least 12 inches deep.

The outdoor kitchen above incorporates another important element—shade. Where natural shade from trees is scarce, consider building a structure similar to the one shown to keep the chef cool. Add decorative elements to make the nook feel more like a room in the landscape, and coordinate the color of the pergola with your home to make the areas feel connected. ❧

OUTDOOR FIREPLACE

Gathering around the bonfire is taken to an all-new level with an outdoor fireplace. No longer a venue simply for "s'mores," an outdoor fireplace can become the defining feature of an open-air living space. This landscape feature is especially welcome in mild climates, where it can be enjoyed practically yearround to take the chill out of the evenings.

When designing an outdoor fireplace, seek the advice of a professional to help create a fireplace that fits with the style of your home, so it looks as though it has always been there. Choose materials with an eye to those used in construction of the house or other landscape features. For instance, this fireplace, with its stucco exterior and tile accents, harmonizes beautifully with the adobe walls and tile roof of the house.

As you plan an outdoor fireplace, take into account the space you will need for furniture and decorative elements. This fireplace is tied to the patio with a low wall, which defines the area and serves as extra seating. Remember that large potted plants can require a fair amount of space but are worth the investment, as they will soften the lines of the fireplace and give it a natural feel. ❧

Building a Garden Playhouse

A playhouse can be a fantasy retreat for children or for adults who wish to recapture a bit of their youth. While the kids may use it for hours of imaginative play, parents can enjoy it for watching wildlife or simply getting a new perspective on life.

When you create a play space for children, consider the type of equipment you want to include. There is a vast array out there, from good old swings and slides to more elaborate gyms. You can build equipment from scratch, or purchase something prefabricated. Some companies will even send a construction team to your home to assemble the structure.

Give some thought to situating the play space in the landscape. Choose a spot that will be visible from inside the house, so you can keep an eye on the children when you are indoors. Position the play equipment so it does not monopolize the entire yard, but rather allows adequate space for gardens, entertaining, and lawn games. If possible, site the play area so it receives shade to make it more enticing in the heat of summer.

On the following pages, learn how to build the simple playhouse featured in the photo at left. ❧

RAISED PLAYHOUSE

This rustic playhouse is easy to build. The sunken 2 x 8-foot runway allows easy access to a slide. ❧

HAVE ON HAND:

For framing:
- Six 8-foot 2 x 8s
- Two 2-foot 2x8s

For posts:
- Six 14-foot 4x4s

For joists:
- Three 8-foot 2x8s
- Three 2-foot 2x8s

For flooring:
- Twenty 8-foot pieces of 6-inch cedar decking

For sides:
- One 4x4-foot and four 4x8-foot panels of lattice
- Seven 4-foot 8-inch 2x4s

- Fifteen 4-foot 2x4s
- Three 8-foot 2x6s
- One 10-foot 2x6
- 12 joist hangers
- Forty-four 3-inch galvanized lag bolts with washers
- 8d and 16d galvanized nails
- Slide and ladder
- Stain or paint
- Level
- Hammer
- Framing square
- Power drill
- Wrench

Dig six 3-foot-deep holes for support posts: one at each corner of the 8 x 10-foot area, and one 2 feet in on each of the 10-foot sides.

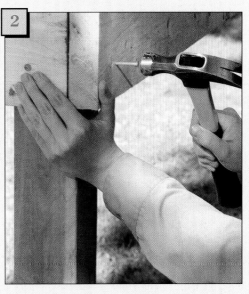

Set posts in concrete. Frame the 8 x 8-foot floor with 2 x 8s. Frame the 2 x 8-foot section 8 inches lower than the main floor.

Use joist hangers to attach three 2 x 8 joists evenly spaced across each area of the frame.

Nail cedar decking over the joists on both the main floor and the extension.

Bolt 2 x 4 uprights at corners and spaced 2 feet apart around sides to support the lattice and railing.

From inside, nail lattice panels to uprights; leave opening for slide and ladder. Attach a 2 x 6 railing all around.

Attach the ladder and slide, following manufacturer's directions.

Go over the entire structure carefully to remove splinters or exposed nails or screws. Finish with stain or paint.

HERE'S HOW

ATTACHING A ROOF

A simple roof will provide shade and shelter from the elements for the playhouse. It covers the 8 x 8-foot part of the playhouse, while leaving the 2 x 8 runway section open for children using the sliding board. You will need 40 feet of 2 x 4 lumber to make rafters for the roof, and an 8-foot-long piece of 2 x 8 for the center support beam. Plan for four rafters for each side of the roof— one on either end, and two equally spaced in between. Notch each rafter so it will sit on the railing, and toenail it into the center support beam. Cover the rafters with exterior-grade plywood to provide a nailing surface for the roofing material. Shingle the roof with naturally rot-resistant cedar shakes, which will weather to a rustic silver-gray.

Alternatives

ADDING A ROOF

Installing a roof over your playhouse will allow you to enjoy it even when the weather is inclement, plus it will help to protect the structure from the elements and preserve it for years to come.

A pitched roof, as shown in the photograph, looks better and is easier to waterproof than a flat roof. But constructing a pitched roof requires a bit more carpentry know-how to get the angles right. Be sure the roof hangs over the walls by several inches, to protect the structure from water runoff. To waterproof a pitched roof, cover it first with plywood, then tar paper, and shingles or other roofing material.

You may also note that this particular tree house is built among several trees, rather than in just one. If you plan to use several trees, be careful when positioning supports for the tree house, because the movement of the trees in the wind could damage the tree house. The easiest way to do this is to fix one end of a support beam to one trunk or branch, and then attach the other end of the beam in a sliding joint (such as a J-shaped metal bracket). When either trunk moves, the support slides across the joint, reducing stress on the tree house. ✤

A TREELESS TREE HOUSE

It isn't necessary to have large trees, or any trees at all, in order to enjoy the benefits of a tree house. A tree house can be constructed simply using poles set in the ground.

When building a tree house that is supported by poles, it is a good idea to secure the poles into the ground with concrete so they can't sink or become loose. The higher you wish to build your tree house, the deeper your poles should be set into the ground. Dig holes where the posts should go, set the posts in the holes, and fill the holes with concrete. When the concrete has set, cover it with soil and grass to create a more finished look.

As this photo illustrates, it isn't necessary to have rigid walls that surround a tree house. Try living walls instead: Train vines to grow up and around the tree house, and situate tall plants nearby to create natural seclusion.

Furnish your tree house to reflect your personality and taste, as you would any room in the house. Here, netting creates a tropical feel for a loft that's as much a romantic getaway for Mom and Dad as it is an exotic hangout for the kids. ✤

A Hammock in the Shade

There's no better way to spend a lazy summer afternoon than in a shaded hammock, as cool breezes gently rock you to sleep.

No longer are hammocks the uncomfortable rope affairs that you'd much rather look at than lounge in. Today's hammocks come in a wide range of styles, materials, and prices. And if you'd prefer to have some company as you relax, there are hammocks that are large enough to handle an entire family.

If your yard doesn't have two trees large enough or close enough together from which to hang a hammock, you can hang it from poles instead. Use two poles, or one pole and a tree. Poles should be 10-foot-long pieces of 4 x 4 lumber. Sink them at least 3½ to 4 feet into the ground, and firmly tamp the soil around the base of the post or fill the holes with quick-setting concrete. Attach the hammock to the posts with either J-hooks or eye bolts that go all the way through the posts. Make the posts part of the landscape by training vines to grow up them, incorporating them into an arbor, or hanging a bird feeder or other garden ornament from them. ❧

HANGING A HAMMOCK

Hanging a hammock between two trees using rope, instead of hooks that are screwed into the trees, will allow you to take your hammock wherever your travels lead you. It is also a method that is kinder to the trees. Use double-braided nylon rope, which is easy to find at home centers. And remember to take the rope and the hammock down at the end of the season to protect both from the elements. ❦

HAVE ON HAND:

▶ Tape measure

▶ Utility knife

▶ Two 15-foot lengths of double-braided nylon rope (more for trees larger than 5 feet around)

▶ Two S-hooks

▶ Hammock

▶ Cool drink

▶ Good book

Choose trees about 12 feet apart. Cut rope long enough to wrap around tree twice, plus at least 5 feet, depending on distance between trees.

With rope centered on tree, wrap rope around tree 4 feet above ground, making an overhand knot on back side of tree (away from hammock).

Bring the two rope ends to the front and tie them in a fisherman's knot or other secure knot. Insert the S-hook into the loop of rope.

Hang the hammock by slipping its end loops into the S-hooks. Climb aboard and relax.

Bringing Features to Light

Do you rush home after work to enjoy a few stolen moments in the garden before the sun slips away? Strategically placed outdoor lighting allows you to linger longer on a summer night to enjoy the scenery as you sit or stroll. Or perhaps you'd like to look out on your garden during winter, but darkness falls so early. Lighting can help to draw your focus outdoors after sundown to enjoy your garden in the off-season.

The size of your garden dictates what types of lights work best. Small gardens with compact trees can use low-voltage lighting. These small-scale fixtures can be mounted on spikes so they can be moved and tucked into beds unobtrusively. You generally plug such systems into regular 120-volt household current. They are widely available in kits that include step-by-step installation instructions. For larger landscapes that require standard-voltage equipment, enlist professional help, especially if the lighting will be located in or near water. Choose lighting equipment carefully, and remember, you get what you pay for.

Outdoor lighting can transform your landscape into a magical new world after the sun goes down and make it much safer in the process, as you will see in the projects on the following pages. ❧

Illuminating Your Walkway

The entryway to your home is often the first thing visitors notice upon arriving. With a simple lighting scheme using a decorative low-voltage lighting system, you can make the path to your door not only welcoming, but safe, too.

Choose low fixtures that cast soft pools of light downward for attractive and functional entryway illumination. By incorporating the lights into the gardens along the path, you can also highlight special features and plants in the landscape by night. Those same plants can help to hide the fixtures by day. Low fixtures can also help to highlight steps. Another option to consider for lighting steps is to use fixtures built into the risers or into a retaining wall on either side of the steps. Both these lighting options, however, require the expertise of an electrician. Staggering lights on either side of the walkway or in a gentle curve can help eliminate the "runway" effect and make the lighting scheme appear more natural.

Low-voltage lighting systems use 12-volt wire and lamps. They are fairly inexpensive and easy to install and do not require special grounding hardware. They connect to the electrical system in your house. ❧

INSTALLING LOW-VOLTAGE LIGHTING

Low-voltage decorative fixtures draw attention to the path leading to the front door. The lights are also strategically placed to guide visitors around the gentle curves in the path. These fixtures are made of special materials to resist weather and coated with an attractive, natural-looking finish. In a low-voltage or 12-volt system, the wire connects to a transformer, which, in turn, plugs into regular 120-volt household current via an outdoor, grounded electrical outlet. ❧

HAVE ON HAND:

- Lighting kit
- Wooden stakes
- Sledgehammer
- String
- Wire cutters
- Needle-nose pliers
- Phillips screwdriver
- Flathead screwdriver

Lay out the pieces of your lighting kit to make sure you have everything. Decide where you want to install the lights and run the cable.

Hammer in stakes to mark places for lights, the first no more than 10 feet from outdoor electrical outlet. Mark cable's route with string.

Install transformer, which is housed in a waterproof casing, at least a foot off the ground in a sheltered location within 1 foot of outlet.

Unroll and lay cable along route where lights will be installed. Be sure to leave some slack in the cable in order to attach it to lights.

Install the first fixture securely in the ground in the desired position. Firm the soil around the base of the light.

Securely fasten cable to transformer according to kit instructions, then attach cable to first light, taking care not to pinch or kink cable.

Install remaining lights along pathway; attach cable to each. Screw in light bulbs; check to see that lights are properly wired and in position.

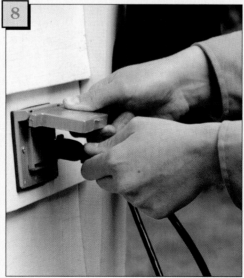

When all lights are in place, plug lighting system into outlet. Adjust fixtures at night to highlight entry features.

HERE'S HOW

CAMOUFLAGING CABLE

The beauty of low-voltage lighting systems is that the cable can be either buried or simply snaked along the ground. If you choose to leave the cable above ground, be sure it is tucked away so no one will trip over it, then cover it with mulch. If you decide to bury the cable in a trench, run it through 1-inch flexible polyethylene pipe to protect the cable.

To run pipe under a walkway, dig on both sides of the walkway. Drive an iron pipe through the ground under the walkway with a sledgehammer. Push polyethylene pipe through the hole as you pull the pipe out the other side.

Whether you bury the cable or leave it above ground, be sure to sketch its location in relation to permanent plantings and other fixtures for future reference.

Alternatives

LAMPPOST LIGHTING

A lamppost can provide an elegant way to add light to a walkway. It is especially useful when placed near an entryway or set at the end of a path. A lamppost serves as a beacon to visitors, safely lights the path to the house, and provides a decorative element to the landscape.

When choosing a lamppost select a light that harmonizes with the rest of your outdoor lighting fixtures and complements the style of your house, yard, or garden. For lampposts placed near the house keep in mind the size of your entryway, and choose a lamppost of the appropriate scale. For fixtures at the end of the walkway select a style that accents nearby gardens or structures. It will be necessary to run underground electrical cable to the lamppost site. Be sure the post is set in concrete or otherwise securely mounted.

Once installed a lamppost should be tastefully accented. Lampposts near the house can be accented with a small welcoming display of perennials that circle the base of the post. Lampposts set away from the house look best when surrounded with tall perennials such as lilies and echinacea. A lamppost is also a wonderful support for climbing vines such as clematis or jasmine. ❧

DOWNLIGHTING AN ENTRYWAY

If you have a place to mount fixtures from above, consider downlighting your entryway as well as the path to your front door. Downlighting highlights a larger area than lights installed along the path, as detailed on the previous pages. This technique accentuates any landscaping around the path and softly lights the walkway. Downlighting also looks more natural, because we are used to seeing light coming down from the sun or moon above. It makes entry safe as well as inviting.

Use floodlights, which cast a wide beam. Mount them under the eaves of your home or from a tall tree that is close to the walkway. You may want to install a timer or motion sensor on this type of light, so you don't have to switch the light on and off. Carefully select the wattage of the light, so it does not dominate the lighting scheme throughout the rest of the landscape. Angle lights so they do not cast a glare for drivers or persons using the path and do not reflect harshly off nearby walls, windows, or water features. To add an interesting effect, position the fixtures so their light is filtered through the leaves below. ❧

Creating Dramatic Lighting

Whether you are indoors or out, you can enjoy the special effects created by an artful array of well-placed lights. One technique that can enhance your illuminated display is uplighting, the act of placing lights at or just above ground level and directing their beams upward to emphasize decking, walls, fences, or garden ornaments. The most dramatic use of uplighting is when those lights are focused on a large or sculptural tree.

Uplighting accentuates the form of a tree, especially a deciduous tree (one that loses its leaves) in winter. This technique takes on a different, more dappled effect when the tree is covered with foliage. When selecting a tree to uplight, consider how that tree looks yearround.

Of course, the best lighting plan incorporates a balance of uplighting, downlighting, and sidelighting. Downlighting, or shining light from a fixture mounted from above, adds fill light and can also be used to accent landscape features. Because sidelighting highlights texture, you can use it to create spectacular shadows on nearby vertical surfaces. Uplighting a tree is the perfect place to begin shedding light on your landscape and is a simple way to bring some theatrics to the nighttime view. 🌿

UPLIGHTING TREES

This simple lighting scheme is suitable for a modest-sized tree and requires three low-voltage lights for the best effect. Using only one light makes the tree appear one-dimensional, without depth or texture. Low-voltage lights are widely available and are small and unobtrusive, so they can be tucked into the garden beds surrounding the tree. A larger tree may require more lights or the intensity of standard-voltage equipment, which is more difficult to install. 🌾

HAVE ON HAND:

▶ 3 accent lights

▶ 12-gauge cable

▶ Transformer

▶ Tape measure

▶ Phillips screwdriver

▶ Flathead screwdriver

▶ Lawn edger

▶ Mulch

▶ Shovel

Select a tree with an interesting form or branching pattern, and one that can be viewed from indoors when lit.

Choose where to locate the transformer. Hang it on a deck, fence, or wall at least 1 foot off the ground and within a foot of an outdoor receptacle.

Measure total length of cable needed to reach from transformer to tree. Do not connect 12-gauge cable to more than 250 watts of lighting.

To visually connect the tree's canopy to the ground, position a fixture so it casts light on the trunk when viewed from a main vantage point.

Position a second fixture so its beam travels up the bare trunk and bathes the canopy in a soft wash of light. Position a third fixture behind tree.

Run cable to each fixture, allowing enough slack so you can reposition lights. Attach light fixtures to cable using manufacturer's connectors.

Turn on lights at dusk; reposition fixtures for best effect. Adjust so they do not shine into your eyes or create "hot spots" on branches.

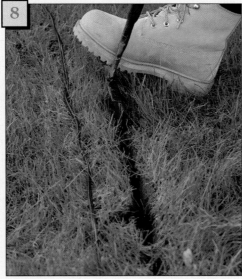

With lawn edger, make trough through sod or mulch. Carefully place the cable in trough. Cover the cable with sod or mulch.

HERE'S HOW

TRANSFORMER SIZE

To figure out what size transformer you need for your lighting scheme, make a list of all the lighting fixtures that will be tapping off the transformer. Add the wattage of each individual fixture together for the total wattage of the lighting plan. Then, purchase a transformer with more capacity than required, but no more than twice the total wattage load you calculated. That way, as you discover other areas you would like to illuminate, you can add a few more lights to the landscape without having to purchase a new transformer.

Alternatives

LIGHTING A WATER GARDEN

A garden pool comes to life at night when lights are incorporated into the design. You will be surprised at the intrigue and mystery you can add to the landscape with a few simple lights strategically placed to illuminate this special feature. Here, a very small investment will deliver a big payoff. As the light plays across the water, its beam is magnified, and the lighted area seems larger.

If you are positioning the lights above and outside the water garden, installation is simple, and low-voltage fixtures will be fine. If, however, you would like to locate the light in the water, as in this photo, you will need to enlist the help of a professional. Position lights to play across the water, accent a group of water-loving plants, or draw attention to a waterfall.

You can also highlight a water garden indirectly, rather than focusing lights directly on the water. Choose a landscape feature nearby, such as a tree, a piece of statuary, or interesting stonework. By training the beam of a small spotlight to shine upward on the feature you have chosen, the light will reflect on the water's surface, and the water garden will be bathed in a gentle rippling glow. ❧

AMBIENT STRING LIGHTS

Strings of lights can provide additional ambiance for outdoor entertaining. You can install them at the last minute and use them to bring a soft glow to areas of the landscape that are otherwise left in the dark.

Both the range and choices of string lights are limitless, so use your imagination when choosing and arranging them in trees and shrubs. For a get-together with a sense of humor, you could bedeck a prize topiary as you would a Christmas tree, complete with multicolored lights that blink. Or consider hanging some novelty string lights to carry the theme of a party, from illuminated chili peppers to paper Japanese lanterns. Don't overlook the standard miniature white lights. Their soft twinkle will add an enchanting glow to any gathering.

Keep in mind that most string lights do not provide enough light to illuminate walkways or other areas safely; they are only a temporary measure to provide atmosphere. Plug extension cords for lights into GFCI outlets, and run them out of the way of traffic. You may even want to secure the cords to the patio or other solid surface with duct tape to prevent tripping. ❧

Distinctive Spaces

One of the greatest joys of working with your landscape is creating features that express your personality. In your garden, you can live out your childhood fantasies of hidden chambers and mysterious passageways by making a secret garden room surrounded by trees. If you find water soothing, you can install a pond that's home to fish and water-loving plants or just create the illusion and beauty of a waterway with a dry streambed. Indulge your culinary ambitions with a raised bed full of fragrant herbs. You can even create a wildlife haven where birds, butterflies, and other creatures find the shelter, food, and water they need.

As you plan a unique space for your landscape, consider ways to get the most pleasure from it. For example, you might tuck your secret nook in a far corner where you can't hear the phone ring, or you might locate the pond near the back door so you can get to it easily and even see it from indoors. If you plan to spend much time in this space, make sure it's livable: Consider the amount of sun it gets, especially in regions with hot summers. Furnish it with comfortable seating. Accent it with personal touches such as wind chimes. And keep the scale in line with the amount of time you have to care for the spot, so you'll have time to enjoy it.

Making a Secret Garden

Hidden places don't lose their appeal just because you've grown up. A secret garden can still be a pleasurable place to retreat by yourself or with a few friends. It doesn't take much to carve out a private nook in a landscape. You can plant fast-growing shrubs to provide a wall, prune existing trees to create a ceiling, and add a layer of mulch to serve as a floor that defines the boundaries of the outdoor room.

As you would with any room, furnish your secret place with comfortable furniture, suited to outdoor use, and decorations such as mirrors, stone sculptures, and perhaps scented herbs or a birdbath. If you decide to add a pond, prevent pesky mosquitoes by installing an aerator or pump to keep the water circulating or introduce fish to prey on insect pests.

When selecting a site for your secret garden, look for a location buffered from traffic noise that has good air circulation. Ideally, the spot will already have established plantings to shelter at least one side and the top of the room. If none exists, you can plant them. While waiting for the plants to fill in, consider growing vines on a simple trellis to screen the secret garden from the rest of the yard. ❧

PLANTING A GARDEN ROOM

This garden room in the far corner of the yard was created using mulch, and a few planted shrubs, along with careful pruning of existing trees and shrubs. Be whimsical with your secret garden by adding garden mirrors, windsocks, or statuary, or furnish it for kids with a fort, colorful decorations, and kid-sized furniture. ❧

HAVE ON HAND:

- ▶ Rope
- ▶ Garden fork
- ▶ Garden rake
- ▶ Black plastic
- ▶ Pruners
- ▶ Loppers
- ▶ Landscape fabric
- ▶ Landscape timbers
- ▶ Power drill
- ▶ Hammer
- ▶ 2 metal spikes per landscape timber
- ▶ Bark mulch
- ▶ Fast-growing shrubs and low trees

Clear out scrubby undergrowth and prune low or damaged branches from existing plants.

Use a rope to outline the garden. Remove weeds or grass in the area, either by digging them out or by smothering them under black plastic.

If existing shrubs are crowded so closely that air doesn't circulate, prune out some branches or remove the weakest plants.

Cover the ground with landscape fabric and secure with landscape fabric pins. Place landscape timbers on the fabric edge.

Drill a large hole at an angle through the ends of each timber. Hammer spikes through the holes and into the soil to anchor the timbers.

Cover the landscape fabric with bark mulch to a depth of 2 inches. Rake the bark periodically to keep it fresh looking.

HERE'S HOW

FAST-GROWING SHRUBS

To establish the walls of your secret room in just a season or two, choose shrubs that grow quickly. A few possibilities include border privet, butterfly bush, red osier dogwood, loropetalum, and tamarisk. Another possibility in sunny areas is to plant tall ornamental grasses such as miscanthus and pampas grass.

Plant vigorous evergreen shrubs and small trees along one or more sides of the area. Dig each hole as deep and twice as wide as nursery pot.

Set plants in a staggered pattern at the edge of the timbers, alternating short plants with taller ones to produce a natural-looking screen.

Alternatives

DARK SECRETS

To add an aura of mystery to a garden, fill it with mysterious plants—those that have dark leaves or flowers or reveal their fragrance only as you draw near them or brush against them.

Certain types of plants are known for their dark leaves. A few of the many dark-leaved coral bells are 'Checkers', 'Chocolate Ruffles', and 'Plum Pudding'. Many coleuses have dark leaves, as do some varieties of ajuga, such as 'Chocolate Chip'. No flowers are truly black, but some are a dark purple—for example, the Darwin tulip 'Queen of the Night', and some species of fritillaria.

Scent also adds mystery, especially if you can't be sure where it's coming from. The sweet smell of lily of the valley wafts for several feet from the flowers. Anise hyssop has a licorice fragrance. Creeping thyme and pineapple weed, when planted between steppingstones, release their aroma when you step on them.

To enjoy the flowers and fragrance of your secret garden, hide a bench or chair nearby that blends into the surroundings. A stone bench is camouflaged near a rock path, while a wooden bench blends into a woodland. ❧

CREATING SECLUSION

You don't need a huge yard to enjoy secret and special garden spaces. Create a sense of seclusion by making the best of blocked lines of sight and carving out separate areas.

A secret space does not have to be completely hidden, just blocked from view from at least one line of sight—perhaps from the house, the driveway, or the neighbors. You might find such a place behind a large tree or at a corner of the garden.

You can establish a sense of seclusion by using plants to create an island. Surround a small patio or circle of lawn with hostas, lilyturf, or other no-fuss plants. You can leave a break in the circle as an entryway, or enclose it completely to reinforce the feeling of being separated from the rest of the yard. A large island, such as a patio, can comfortably contain a table and several chairs. But even a little flower-surrounded nook can hold a small bench or glider.

To complete the sense of seclusion, add a focal point, such as a fountain or birdbath, that you might be able to see or hear easily only when you're in that special spot. ❧

Adding a Water Feature

A water garden can encompass anything from a simple tub to a moving stream complete with waterfall and fish-filled pond. On whatever scale you choose to build your water garden, it can be a delightful, cool oasis that reflects images, attracts wildlife, and supports beautiful water-loving plants.

Such a dominant landscape feature might seem like an elaborate undertaking, but flexible liners and preformed ponds make it simple to create a natural-looking pond. A pond supply dealer can help you choose a long-lasting, durable liner suited to your climate and needs.

A pond can become the focal point of the yard, so locate it where you can best enjoy it. You might want to be able to see it from a particular window, from the deck, or as you enter the house. Placing the pond where it is shaded during the afternoon helps prevent algae. If no shade is available, you can also prevent algae by darkening the water every 4 to 6 weeks with an inexpensive, nontoxic pond dye or by heavily planting the pond with floating and submerged plants.

If the pond you install is larger than 10 x 10 feet or if you will be adding fish, you'll need to plumb and wire the pond for a submersible pump and filter. ❧

IN-GROUND POCKET POND

This pond is formed with a flexible plastic pond liner. For a more natural look, grow marginal plants in pots on a shallow ledge and place stones on the outer rim to conceal the liner. It is most important that the excavated edge is level all the way around so that the pond fills evenly. If possible, work on a sunny day, so the liner is more pliable. 🌿

HAVE ON HAND:

- ▶ Hose or rope
- ▶ Spray paint
- ▶ Spade
- ▶ Tape measure
- ▶ 2 x 4
- ▶ Carpenter's level
- ▶ Sand
- ▶ Single-piece pond liner
- ▶ Scissors
- ▶ Stones
- ▶ Hose connected to water supply

Outline pond area with rope or hose, and then mark outline with spray paint. Remove sod from area with a spade.

Dig a ledge 9 inches deep and wide around the marked area. Dig center 18 inches deep, sloping sides 45°. Remove large, sharp stones.

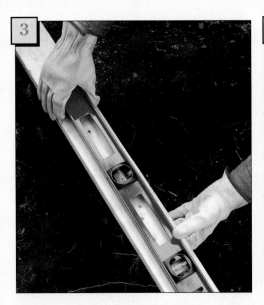

Place a 2 x 4 across the pond and use a carpenter's level to check that the edges are level all around. Add or remove soil as needed.

Use this formula to calculate liner size:
Liner width = width + (depth x 2) + (overlap x 2).
Liner length = length + (depth x 2) + (overlap x 2).

Cover sides and bottom of area with about 2 inches of moist sand. Place folded liner in center of hole.

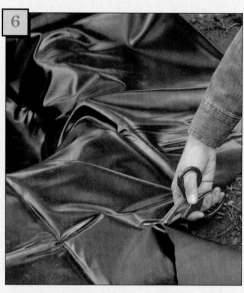

Unfold liner to cover floor of pond, folding it to fit curves. Use scissors to trim liner if needed, leaving 1 foot extra for overlap all around the edge.

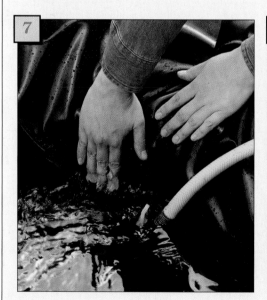

Use a hose to fill pond with water, gently stretching the liner to remove large creases. Secure the liner's overlap with stones.

Fill with water to about 2 inches from the top. Trim liner edge to 6 to 8 inches and cover with flat stones to conceal.

HERE'S HOW

ADDING FISH AND PLANTS

Introduce fish a few at a time so the pond's ecology can adjust to the changes the fish will cause. Goldfish and koi are the most widely used pond fish. In general, a pond can support 1 inch of fish body length for every 2 square feet of pond surface. To keep fish as healthy as possible, install a pump with a biological filter. Check pH daily; it should be between 7 and 8.5.

To add interest to the pond and keep the water free from algae, grow enough plants to cover one-half to three-quarters of the water surface with leaves. Place potted marginal plants, such as cattails and yellow flag iris on the shallow ledge. Grow water lilies and lotus in pots on the bottom. To shade the surface, add floating plants such as water hyacinth and water lettuce. To add oxygen, which is especially important for fish and to control algae, grow submerged plants such as pondweed.

Alternatives

A TUB WATER GARDEN

You don't need a lot of room to have a water garden. You can grow several beautiful water plants in any watertight pot, barrel, or tub. If you have a decorative clay or ceramic planter you want to use, you can place a rigid plastic pot liner in it. Or you can seal it by filling the drainage holes with a waterproof sealant and coating the inside of the pot with the tar used to seal roofs.

In keeping with the container's small scale, use dwarf water plants. First position the plant that needs to be planted deepest, such as a dwarf hardy water lily or dwarf sacred lotus. Plant it in a pot of sand or water-plant potting soil, and cover the soil surface with a layer of pea gravel to keep the soil from floating into the water. Next, set a potted shallow-water plant, such as dwarf papyrus, near the edge of the deep plant's pot. Finally, add a few small floating plants, such as water fern and water hyacinth.

Because a small container water garden cannot support fish, use mosquito dunks, a biological control, to keep mosquitoes from breeding in the pond. Add water to the container each week to compensate for evaporation. ❧

GARDENS IN WATER

A pond gives you the opportunity to grow water-loving plants that can't survive on dry land. Grow a variety of plants, both to ensure an attractive array of textures and bloom times and to keep the pond's ecology in balance.

Water plants fall into four groups: deep-water, marginal, submerged, and floating. Deep-water plants are the big-flowered show-stoppers, like water lilies and lotus. Grow them in 14-quart pots in 24 to 48 inches of water. Marginal plants, sometimes called bog or shallow-water plants, thrive in the soggy soil at the edge of a pond. A few examples are cattails, yellow flag iris, and marsh marigolds. Grow marginals in pots set on a shallow shelf around the pond's edge. The surface of the pot should be at or just below the water surface.

Submerged plants grow completely below the surface. This group includes pondweed, and eel grass. They add oxygen that fish need and prevent algae.

Floating plants, such as water hyacinth and water lettuce, drift in the water, their roots floating freely. Floaters and the floating leaves of deep-water plants should cover about three-quarters of the water surface. ❧

Building a Bed for Herbs

A raised bed solves many common gardening problems. Improved soil drainage means plant roots are healthier because they aren't surrounded by excess water. The soil in a raised bed warms faster in the spring. As a result, you can plant earlier, and established perennial plants start growing more quickly. If your soil is difficult to work because it is rocky and high in clay, you can literally rise above the problem and fill the raised bed with good soil.

Raised beds can be almost any height, from a few inches to several feet. Low beds are best for hot, dry regions, where good drainage and warm soil can be too much of a good thing. Tall beds are a good option for growing deep-rooted trees and shrubs. They also make gardening easier for people who have difficulty kneeling and bending.

Cedar and cypress are good choices for wooden raised beds because they resist rot. The use of pressure-treated lumber near food crops, such as the herbs in this garden, is controversial, because chemicals used to treat it can leach into the soil. A better choice would be plastic lumber.

BUILDING A RAISED BED

These instructions are for a bed with four straight sides, set within an existing walkway. The bed in the photo uses 2 x 6s. You can use a wider board for a higher bed. ❧

HAVE ON HAND:

- ▶ Spade or garden fork
- ▶ Tape measure
- ▶ Circular saw
- ▶ Power drill and bits
- ▶ Eight 3-inch wood screws
- ▶ Framing square
- ▶ Screwdriver
- ▶ Four 4-inch L-brackets with screws

- ▶ Eight 1-inch wood screws
- ▶ Carpenter's level
- ▶ Topsoil-compost mix
- ▶ Slow-release fertilizer
- ▶ Garden rake

Cutting List
- ▶ Four 2 x 8 boards, cut to fit

Use a spade or garden fork to till the ground 3 inches deep, removing large rocks, twigs, and other debris.

Measure the 2 long sides of the bed and cut two 2 x 8s to fit. Measure and cut boards for 2 shorter sides to fit between the longer boards.

Butt a short board to the inside of a long board. Drill 2 pilot holes and join boards with 3-inch wood screws. Join each corner in same manner.

Attach corner brackets to the inside of each corner to strengthen the frame. Drill pilot holes and attach brackets with 1-inch wood screws.

Set the frame in place over the prepared bed. Use a carpenter's level and check all sides to be sure they are level.

If frame is not level, remove or add soil from beneath portions of the frame until plumb.

Fill the bed with a mixture of compost and top-soil. Add slow-release fertilizer to the soil mixture per label instructions.

Smooth the soil with a rake into a low mound that is highest in the center and lowest along the edges.

HERE'S HOW

CURVING AN EDGE

For a low raised bed that accommodates a curved walkway, end the wooden portion where the walk begins to curve. Then dig a shallow trench along the curved edge of the walkway. Make the trench as wide as the thickness of a brick and deep enough that the top of the brick is level with the top of the boards when the brick is set on end in the trench. Place the bricks into the trench, then fill any gaps with soil and press the soil firmly into place.

Alternatives

A BRICK RAISED BED

Brick gives the bed a sense of formality and permanence that wooden timbers don't. Brick raised beds are a good choice for the front of brick and clapboard houses like Cape Cods, colonials, and ranches (for contemporary houses, cabins, and houses with cedar siding, wooden timbers are better suited). In addition to herbs and perennials, include a mix of low shrubs and ornamental grasses so the bed holds interest yearround. A few options include cotoneaster, dwarf hollies, red-stemmed dogwood, dwarf conifers, blue fescue, and giant feather grass.

Brick beds are easy to construct. Use frostproof bricks, which are more durable than facing bricks. Prepare a concrete footing for the wall; it should be deep enough that the top of the first course of bricks is at soil level. Leave the surface of the concrete footing rough, so mortar clings to it better. Once the concrete has cured, begin laying the bricks, using masonry mortar to set them. Check often to make sure the bricks are level. Leave unmortared gaps between some bricks in the first course above soil level, so excess water can drain from the bed. ❧

EASY-ACCESS RAISED BED

Tall raised beds make gardening possible for those who can't easily bend to ground level. When properly designed, the beds make tasks such as planting, watering, weeding, and harvesting manageable.

The most appropriate design depends on the gardener. For those who can't stoop or kneel for long periods, a bed that's 24 to 27 inches high and has a wide rim to sit on can be a good solution. For gardeners in wheelchairs, 27 inches is usually a good height.

While tall raised beds can be any length, they should be narrow enough that the gardener can reach the center from either side. Depending on the gardener's strength and flexibility, that might be as wide as 4 feet or as narrow as 2 feet.

Sturdy construction is critical for a tall raised bed. Wide landscape timbers are a popular choice for deep raised beds. For reinforcement, insert sturdy iron rods vertically through predrilled holes in each corner and at intervals along the sides. Surround the beds with a level surface that's easy to negotiate, such as a wide paved walkway. ❧

Creating a Dry Streambed

You can use a wet, low-lying problem area (also called a swale) to your landscape's advantage. Even if it's not wet, you can create the illusion of a stream running through your property by filling the area with stones. Besides adding the feeling of moving water, a swale filled with attractive stones provides a visual break to divide a large expanse of yard. You can also use it to direct the eye toward an interesting feature or as a barrier across a route that you don't want people taking. If your yard has a gully where rainwater runs off, a stone-filled streambed can be a practical solution as well as a decorative feature. The rocks that line the gully slow the flow of heavy rains. They also prevent water from striking soil directly and jolting it loose.

For the most natural effect, choose stone native to your area. The color of rock you choose and the depth to which you fill the bed help create the illusion. Use bluish rocks to simulate smooth water and white rocks for rushing water. Fill the bed so the surface is level, as it would be if filled with water. For a dry streambed, use river rock of various tones; the rocks should follow the curved floor of the streambed. ❀

INSTALLING A SWALE

This swale has a concave surface, to resemble a dry streambed. It uses washed river rocks, which are smooth, colorful stones from streambeds. Stones are sold by size; the ones used for this project are 2 to 3 inches wide. Unless your streambed is small, buy rock in bulk from a stone yard, rather than by the bag from a home improvement warehouse. The amount of rock you need will vary, depending on the depth, width, and length of the swale. ❦

HAVE ON HAND:

▶ Hose or heavy rope

▶ Spray paint or flour

▶ Shovel or spade

▶ Scissors

▶ Landscape fabric

▶ Landscape fabric pins

▶ Washed river rock

▶ Accent rocks

▶ Perennials and shrubs

Use a hose or heavy rope to outline the swale, forming a natural, gently curving shape. Mark outline with spray paint or flour.

Remove weeds and other plants, including lawn turf, from the outlined area.

If the area is flat, dig it out so that it is about 6 inches deep in the center, tapering up to ground level at the edges.

Cover the area with landscape fabric to suppress future weeds. Cut the fabric to fit, and secure with landscape fabric pins.

Place larger stones along the edge of the land-scape fabric to conceal and anchor it.

Arrange some additional large stones inside the area, as accents. You can space them, if desired, to suggest steppingstones.

Fill the area with a 3-inch-deep layer of washed river stones.

Plant perennials and shrubs, such as daylilies and rhododendron, in clusters along rock border and among groupings of stone.

HERE'S HOW

PLANTS FOR AN ARROYO

Plants along the edge of a swale help it seem more natural, blending it with the rest of the landscape. If your swale is usually dry, with short wet spells, grow plants that can tolerate the cycle of wet and dry, such as 'Autumn Joy' sedum and maiden grass. If your swale is just for decoration and you want to mimic a southwestern arroyo, grow plants with leathery or gray-green leaves; possibilities include Russian sage and rosemary.

Alternatives

CHANNELING WATER

A swale is an attractive and practical solution for long, sloping areas where water rushes after heavy or prolonged rains. The stones in the swale slow the flow of water. They also protect topsoil from washing away and leaving an ugly ditch. And because stones dry more quickly than bare soil, there's no mud to track into the house.

When making the swale, start with the natural outline of the path the water follows. Use a spade to level off high spots so water doesn't collect there (another option is to make that spot into a little pond by lining it with a pond liner and planting it with bog plants). Adding curves along the water's path will help slow the water. Line it with stones that are 2 inches or bigger—they won't wash away easily. Add some larger stones here and there for a more natural look.

If your swale is often wet, plant moisture-loving plants along its fringe, such as horsetail, ferns, and sweet flag. If it is seldom wet but experiences gully-washers, choose plants that tolerate both wet and dry soil and have strong root systems, such as daylilies and Siberian iris. ❦

STREAMBED PATHWAY

For an interesting twist on a pathway, and one that's well suited to a naturalistic setting, make a path that looks like the serpentine meandering of a stream. Use a rope or rubber hose to mark the area where the path will be; a wide, curving shape looks most natural. Either remove the sod in the marked area or mow it very short. Line the area with landscape fabric to smother the grass and keep future weeds in check. If available, use heavy-duty, nonwoven, sun-bonded landscape fabric (for driveways and sidewalks).

Place flat steppingstones in a meandering line, like you'd find in a natural creek crossing, but space them close enough to walk on comfortably. Then fill the area with attractive stones. They don't have to be large, as they won't actually be stopping flowing water. Combine different sizes to mimic nature. To make your nonactive streambed look more like the real thing, consider ending it with a planting of blue fescue, to suggest a pond. To keep the stones in place, border the streambed pathway with plastic or metal edging. To hide the edging, plant a ground cover, such as lilyturf, along the side. ❦

Making a Wildlife Haven

Watching a bird peek from its birdhouse, a butterfly land on a blossom, or a toad hop from its hiding place adds a new dimension to your enjoyment of your garden. To draw wildlife to your garden, you need only know a little about animals' requirements for food, shelter, and water. For example, most birds prefer feeding in the open but close to cover, such as a shrub, so they can easily escape danger. Some feed at ground level, such as from a pan of seed set on the ground, while others like to perch higher, on a bird feeder. If you install a feeder, choose one that has large and small openings, so that both large and small birds can eat.

If you invite butterflies, be prepared to also welcome their leaf-eating young: caterpillars. Keep a butterfly guide handy to help you identify caterpillars and know what butterflies they'll become. Butterflies are most active when warm, so make sure part of the garden is sunny. In hot climates, they appreciate dappled shade.

To attract insect-eating toads, provide a cool, dark hiding place, such as an inverted flowerpot with one side propped up. Keep the area around the flowerpot moist.

A BIRD AND BUTTERFLY GARDEN

This mix of plants attracts birds, butterflies, and beneficial insects. Because some plants in this garden are perennials that will be in place for years to come, before you plant, have the soil tested to determine what nutrients the soil needs. 🌸

HAVE ON HAND:

- Garden fork or power tiller
- Compost
- Posthole digger
- Power drill
- 8-foot-long 4 x 4 post
- Birdhouse
- Trowel
- Mulch

Plants
- Butterfly bush
- 'Happy Returns' daylily
- 'Coronation Gold' yarrow
- Pyrethrum
- 'Cambridge Scarlet' bee balm
- Red cosmos
- Garden phlox
- Purple and white cone-flowers
- Gayfeather
- Nicotiana
- 'Purple Palace' coral bells
- Lamb's ears

Clear the area of vegetation and loosen soil with a garden fork or power tiller. Spread a 3-inch layer of compost over area and till into soil.

Make an 18-inch-deep hole and set the post in it. Attach the birdhouse to the post.

Plant shrubs, such as butterfly bush, first. Set them toward the rear of the garden or a few feet from the birdhouse.

Yellow flowers attract butterflies. Plant bunches of 'Happy Returns' yellow daylilies and 'Coronation Gold' yarrow in center of garden.

Red flowers attract hummingbirds. Plant 'Cambridge Scarlet' bee balm and red cosmos near the yellow flowers.

Nectar plants attract butterflies, hummingbirds, and bees. Plant clumps of garden phlox, cone-flower, gayfeather, and nicotiana.

Near the front of the garden, add plants with textured, colorful foliage, such as 'Purple Palace' coral bells and lamb's ears.

Spread a 3- or 4-inch layer of mulch, such as bark chips, between plants. Keep the mulch about 2 inches from the stems of plants.

HERE'S HOW

PROVIDING WATER

To make it easier for birds to use a birdbath, place a rock in the middle, so that the top of it is about an inch above the water. Change the water often to keep it clean. Birds are also attracted to the sound of running water. To create a splashing sound, hang a water-filled gourd, milk jug, or similar container from a branch or pole. Place a large flat rock, bowl, or birdbath under the container. Punch a little hole in the container to allow a slow drip onto the rock or bowl below.

Butterflies like to drink from moist soil or gravel, for both the water and the salts in the mud. Either keep a patch of bare soil wet for them, or set out a shallow bowl filled with wet sand or stones, sprinkled with Epsom salts.

Alternatives

WILDLIFE-ATTRACTING PLANTS

Different birds and butterflies prefer different plants. Some birds, such as chickadees, prefer plants that produce abundant seeds, like sunflowers. Other birds, including many songbirds, need dense shrubs for hiding places. Some butterflies like gayfeather blooms, while others prefer coneflower. The easiest way to attract wildlife to your garden is to grow a variety of plants with flowers of different sizes and colors that bloom at different times during the growing season. Allow at least some flowers to go to seed, as food for birds. For butterflies, grow plants that provide nectar, such as lilac and impatiens, as well as those that the caterpillars like to eat, including parsley and snapdragons. Remember, too, that wildlife needs not only food from plants but also shelter, so include trees and shrubs in your landscape.

If you're intent on attracting a specific animal, find out if it has a preferred food source. Monarch butterflies, for example, lay their eggs on milkweed. Hummingbirds are attracted to red, tubular flowers.

To protect wildlife, do not use insecticides or other pesticides. Even some organic insecticides, such as Bt, present a hazard. Fortunately, if you grow a variety of plants, you'll attract beneficial insects that will control many insect pests. ❦

BUTTERFLY BUSH
Buddleia spp.
8–12 feet
Zones 5–9
Woody shrub with long, slender branches and lance-shaped gray-green leaves. Sharply scented purple, lilac, red, or white flowers appear in summer to fall. Full sun; fertile, well-drained soil; even moisture.

LANTANA
Lantana camara
3–6 feet
Zones 8–11
Fast-growing, variable plants with aromatic, medium green leaves and often prickly stems. Clusters of tubular purple, red, yellow, or white flowers from spring to fall. Full sun; well-drained, fertile soil; even, moderate moisture.

MEADOW PHLOX
Phlox maculata **'Delta'**
2–3 feet
Zones 5–8
Upright perennial with lance-shaped, medium green leaves. Bears lightly scented violet, pink, or white flowers in spring. Full sun; well-drained, fertile soil; moderate moisture; deadhead flowers to extend flowering; cut back to ground in fall.

GAYFEATHER
Liatris spicata **'Kobold'**
2–3 feet
Zones 4–9
Strong stems lined with narrow, dark green leaves and crowned with spike of small, spidery flowers. Blossoms appear in summer and open from top of spike to bottom. Full sun; light, well-drained, evenly moist soil.

BLACK-EYED SUSAN
Rudbeckia fulgida
2–3 feet
Zones 4–9
Perennial with basal rosette of green, hairy leaves. Pliant stem topped with daisylike yellow flowers accented with dark central eye. Full sun to partial shade; well-drained, moderately fertile organic soil; average moisture.

Glossary

ACID (acidic) a soil with a pH lower than 7.0. Slightly acidic soil is acceptable to most plants. A soil pH below 5.5 is too acidic for many plants.

ALKALINE a soil with a pH higher than 7.0; opposite of acidic soil. Also known as sweet soil.

ANNUAL a plant that sprouts from seed, grows, flowers, sets seed, and dies within a single growing season.

ARBOR a garden structure with a roof and open sides, often with vines trained across the sides and top.

AUGER machine or hand tool used to bore holes in the ground.

BAND SAW a power saw used in woodworking, consisting of a toothed metal band driven around the circumferences of two wheels.

BIENNIAL a plant that begins growth one year and flowers, sets seed, and dies following a dormant period.

CEMENT a powder of lime and other minerals that hardens when combined with water. Used as the binding agent in mortar and concrete.

CIRCULAR SAW a power saw for cutting wood or metal, consisting of a toothed disk rotated at high speed.

CLAY a soil type made up of very small soil particles. Clay soils easily become hard and compacted and may not drain well unless they are improved by adding organic matter.

COMPOST the soft organic material that results from the partial decay of plant matter.

CONCRETE a mixture of cement, sand, crushed stone or gravel, and water used for foundations, steps, paths, and so on.

CROWN the point where roots are joined to aboveground plant parts; also the canopy of a tree.

CULTIVAR a variety of a plant selected and propagated by people.

DECIDUOUS a plant that drops its leaves in fall and produces new foliage in spring.

DIVISION the technique of separating plant clumps into several smaller parts by pulling or cutting apart crowded roots, bulbs, or corms.

DORMANT the "resting" state of a plant, as when perennials die back in winter.

DRAINAGE the movement of water over or through a surface such as soil. The speed of drainage depends on steepness of slope, type of soil, and factors such as compaction.

EROSION the movement of topsoil away from a given site by water or wind.

EVERGREEN a plant that holds its green foliage through multiple growing seasons.

FLAGSTONE a flat stone used in paving, or any rock that will split into such stones.

FOUNDATION the part of a house that rests upon the ground or extends into the ground.

GRADE a term that describes the degree of slope in a given site. Level sites have zero grade. To grade a site means to reshape soil into a very slight slope that helps water drain away from the area.

GROUND COVER any plants, shrubs, or materials planted or placed where grass is not desired or practical. Used to cover steep slopes or rocky terrains, for example.

HARDY describes a plant that survives in a particular climate.

HERBACEOUS a plant that has little or no woody tissue, which in cold climates dies back to the roots each year during winter.

HUMUS decayed organic matter that is added to soil to improve its structure and ability to hold air and water. Compost, peat moss, rotted leaves, weathered straw, composted bark, and rotted sawdust are different types of humus.

LANDSCAPE FABRIC a synthetic fabric that allows water to penetrate into the soil and provides a mechanical barrier to keep weeds from growing in areas such as pathways or up into raised beds.

LATTICE (or latticework) crisscross structure of laths; often used for screens.

LEVEL in carpentry, a board, plank, or other structural part that is perfectly horizontal. A tool called a carpenter's level is used to see whether a line is perfectly horizontal.

LIME a calcium compound usually applied to acidic soil to raise the pH. The type of lime best for gardens, called agricultural or garden lime, is made from ground limestone.

MARGINAL PLANT a plant grown either in shallow water or in moist soil around pool edges and banks of watercourses.

MICROCLIMATE an area within a large climate in which local factors such as shade, moisture, and exposure make it different from the surrounding area.

MITER to make a joint by cutting two pieces of wood at an angle and fitting them together.

MORTAR a mixture of cement and sand used to bind bricks or stones together.

MULCH any material spread over the soil surface to retain soil moisture, moderate soil temperature, and suppress the growth of weeds.

PAVERS special bricks or flat pieces of formed concrete used for constructing walkways. Pavers are usually not as thick as building (or facing) bricks and are made of a dense material so that they resist cracking under pressure.

PEAT MOSS various types of sphagnum moss used as a soil amendment.

PERENNIAL a plant that can live for more than two years.

PERGOLA an arbor covered walk or overhead structure built to give shade or shelter to a patio or deck.

PESTICIDE a substance used to manage pests and diseases. Systemic pesticides are taken up by plants and become part of their physiology; they are not used on edible plants. The label on any pesticide product shows a specific list of plants on which the product may be used as well as the pest or disease it controls. Types of pesticides include insecticides and fungicides.

pH a measure of a soil's acidity or alkalinity on a scale of 1.0 to 14.0, with 7.0 being neutral. A pH below 7.0 is acidic; above 7.0 is alkaline.

PLUMB in carpentry, a post or plank that is perfectly vertical.

PRESSURE-TREATED LUMBER is wood that has been chemically treated under high pressure to protect it from rot, insects, and other sources of decay; wear protection when handling this type of lumber.

PRUNING the process of cutting away unwanted pieces from a plant. Pruning can be done to remove damaged or diseased plant parts, to shape the plant, or to force the plant to send available energy to flowering buds.

RESEED the ability of some plants to shed seeds that successfully germinate and grow.

ROOTBALL the mass of roots and the soil visible when you remove a plant from its pot or ground.

SABER SAW a light, portable electric saw with a pointed, reciprocating blade.

SAND a soil type made up of large, gritty mineral particles. Sandy soils drain quickly and do not hold moisture or nutrients well unless they are improved by the addition of humus.

SOIL HEAVING the forcing of plants, stones, or other materials to the soil surface through alternate freezing and thawing. Affects young plants in particular.

SWALE a low tract of land, especially when moist or marshy.

TENDER a plant susceptible to frost damage.

TOENAIL a nail driven obliquely, as to join vertical and horizontal beams.

TRANSFORMER a device used to transfer electric energy from one circuit to another.

WOODY forming stems that mature to wood.

Index

TIME® LIFE BOOKS

Time-Life Books is a division of Time Life Inc.
Time-Life is a trademark of Time Warner Inc. and affiliated companies.

TIME LIFE INC.

CHAIRMAN AND CHIEF EXECUTIVE OFFICER: Jim Nelson
PRESIDENT AND CHIEF OPERATING OFFICER: Steven Janas
SENIOR EXECUTIVE VICE PRESIDENT AND CHIEF OPERATIONS OFFICER:
    Mary Davis Holt
SENIOR VICE PRESIDENT AND CHIEF FINANCIAL OFFICER: Christopher Hearing

TIME-LIFE BOOKS

PRESIDENT: Larry Jellen
SENIOR VICE PRESIDENT, NEW MARKETS: Bridget Boel
VICE PRESIDENT, HOME AND HEARTH MARKETS: Nicholas M. DiMarco
VICE PRESIDENT, CONTENT DEVELOPMENT: Jennifer L. Pearce

TIME-LIFE TRADE PUBLISHING

VICE PRESIDENT AND PUBLISHER: Neil S. Levin
SENIOR SALES DIRECTOR: Richard J. Vreeland
DIRECTOR, MARKETING AND PUBLICITY: Inger Forland
DIRECTOR OF TRADE SALES: Dana Hobson
DIRECTOR OF CUSTOM PUBLISHING: John Lalor
DIRECTOR OF RIGHTS AND LICENSING: Olga Vezeris

MORE LANDSCAPE PROJECTS

DIRECTOR OF NEW PRODUCT DEVELOPMENT: Carolyn M. Clark
NEW PRODUCT DEVELOPMENT MANAGER: Lori A. Woehrle
SENIOR EDITOR: Linda Bellamy
DIRECTOR OF DESIGN: Kate L. McConnell
PROJECT EDITOR: Jennie Halfant
TECHNICAL SPECIALIST: Monika Lynde
PAGE MAKEUP SPECIALIST: Jennifer Gearhart
DIRECTOR OF PRODUCTION: Carolyn Bounds
QUALITY ASSURANCE: Jim King and Stacy L. Eddy

Printed in U.S.A.
10 9 8 7 6 5 4 3 2 1

Produced by Storey Communications, Inc.
Pownal, Vermont

President	Pamela B. Art
Director of Custom Publishing	Megan Kuntze
Editorial Director	Margaret J. Lydic
Project Manager	Gwen W. Steege
Book Editor	Molly T. Jackel
Horticultural Editor	Charles W.G. Smith
Photo Coordination	Giles Prett, Cici Mulder, Erik Callahan
Book Design	Jonathon Nix/Verso Design
Art Direction	Mark A. Tomasi
Photo Stylist	Sheri Lamers
Production and Layout	Jennifer A. Jepson Smith
Indexer	Nan Badgett/Word·a·bil·ity
Authors	Jill Jesiolowski Cebenko and Erin Hynes
Primary Photography	Kevin Kennefick

Additional photography on pages, as follows: ©Gay Bumgarner (39 right, 61 left); Rob Cardillo (98); ©Walter Chandoha (116); Julie Ann Clayton/H. Armstrong Roberts (109 right); Crandall & Crandall (26, 27, 70, 71, 84, 85, 86, 97 left, 97 right, 104, 105 113 left, 131 left, 131 right); R. Todd Davis (35 right, 50, 119 right); Alan & Linda Detrick (62, 132); ©Ken Druse (28, 47 right, 119 left); ©Derek Fell (Brickman Group Design) (6, 7, 48, 49, 76, 79 right, 80, 90, 93 right, 101 left, 109 left, 123 left); Roger Foley (89 right, 110); ©David Goldberg (44); ©Hammocks, Etc from Eck & Associates (102); Harry Haralambou (47) R. Krubner/H. Armstrong Roberts (93 left); D. Logan/H. Armstrong Roberts (106); Janet Loughrey (101 right, 114, 115); J. Paul Moore (8, 66, 72); Jerry Pavia (32, 35 left, 39 left, 54 right, 61, 89 left, 127 left, 127 right); Positive Images/Gay Bumgarner (79 left); Positive Images/Jerry Howard (iv, v);Giles Prett/Storey Communications, Inc. (cover, 36, 94, 120), K. Rice/H.Armstrong Roberts (40); ©Ron Schramm/gardenIMAGE (128); ©Chuck Savage/Stock Market (109 left); A. Teufen/H. Armstrong Roberts (113 right); Robert Walch (123 right, 124).

Special thanks to the followng for their help: Berkshire Botanical Garden, Stockbridge, MA; California Redwood Association, Novato, CA; Collector's Warehouse, Williamstown, MA; Hammocks, Etc from Eck & Associates (www.hameck.com); Ward's Nursery and Garden Center, Great Barrington, MA.

School and library distribution by Time-Life Education,
P.O. Box 85026, Richmond, Virginia 23285-5026.

CIP data available upon request:
Librarian, Time-Life Books
2000 Duke Street
Alexandria, Virginia 22314

ISBN 0-7370-0625-0

Zone Map

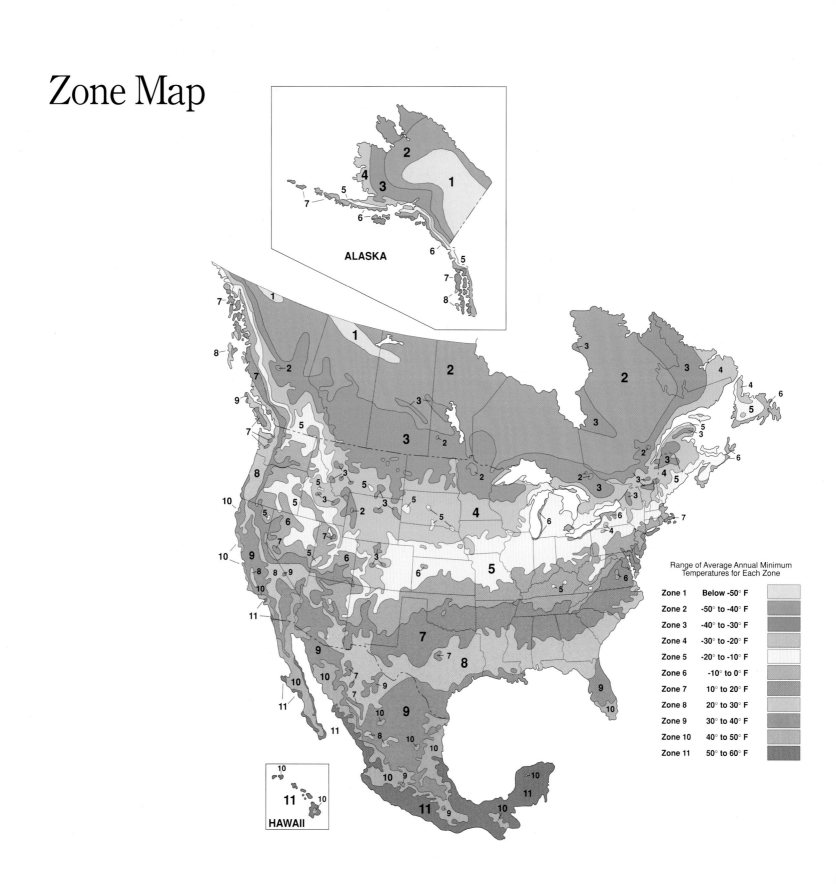

ALASKA

HAWAII

Range of Average Annual Minimum
Temperatures for Each Zone

Zone 1	Below -50° F
Zone 2	-50° to -40° F
Zone 3	-40° to -30° F
Zone 4	-30° to -20° F
Zone 5	-20° to -10° F
Zone 6	-10° to 0° F
Zone 7	10° to 20° F
Zone 8	20° to 30° F
Zone 9	30° to 40° F
Zone 10	40° to 50° F
Zone 11	50° to 60° F